THE MANUAL FC
THE NEW EARTH.

MW01226110

...Mother Earth frequency has changed, and it is accelerating rapidly. The higher frequencies of light are available to all beings.

There is a need for adjustments to our bodies to be in harmony with the current global alteration of consciousness and light.

Together with all planets, stars, galaxies, and universes, we are on the acceleration path.

It is a process of our rebirth and reconstruction...

"Repelling eye-opening and heart-touching— revelations about the current times with a most positive twist, leading to one's inevitable change and transformation."

B. Wein New Age author US

"Your light, love and words spread truth and a vital message, while informing and educating. What you write is inspiring and uplifting and each word is loaded with love for all that has been, is and will ever be. Glorious. "

Fauxcroft poet, UK

"Fascinating insights into natural cycles and the impact on life harmony. You can see nature fluxes around these cycles... somewhere we have lost the connection and rhythm in our Modern society...

Gary J.. Fiction author, UK

TO HUMANITY FOR MASTERING THE PHYSICAL WORLD AND MOVING INTO HIGHER STATES OF CONSCIOUSNESS AND AWARENESS.

The Manual For Humanity Thriving In The New Earth

Knowledge,
Wisdom, and
Practical Techniques
To Mastering The Physical

Tat Jane Bego Vic

Preface

In my sincere desire to feet the need and humanity's process of evolution to the next levels of consciousness and awareness, and the shifts we are experiencing in our new reality, *The Manual For Humanity Thriving In The New Earth* reveals characteristics and traits of the new paradigm on earth.

I am introducing the ancient and new knowledge and practices to assist our necessary recalibration and how best to benefit from these monumental times.

Mother Earth frequency has changed, and it is accelerating rapidly. The higher frequencies of light are available to humanity and all beings. Consequently, we need to make changes to our physical, mental, emotional, and spiritual self to be in tune with this global alteration of consciousness, together with Mother Earth and all planets, stars, galaxies, and universes.

This global reset to higher frequency light consciousness is a process of rebirth and reconstruction for all. Thus, our whole being and life are rearranging, and this time through the heart in the now moment is when we can benefit the most.

Therefore, seeing and understanding that all current events are for our highest benefits, our awakening, and evolving while moving forward, the wisdom and practical techniques I introduced when assimilated and utilized can allow this transfiguration to take place naturally.

The crux for our progress, collectively and individually, is the opening of the heart when we can experience liberation and joy in possibilities for our expansion. Although the reality may not look always that way, indeed, we are to progress in all areas of our lives in this new paradigm.

How is this possible?

Exactly, through a shift from solely the mind to also the heart-based consciousness and awareness, in every moment, we enter the knowledge and harmony within and with the parameters of the New Earth.

The knowledge that reveals this wisdom proceeds from Buddhist, Hindu, and other ancient traditions, I studied through my adulthood. Also, the soul wisdom and practices I focused on while studying with the Institute of Soul Healing and Enlightenment for five years. After a few years of assimilating and implementing all these teachings, I accessed my multidimensional self and being, which practices and wisdom I shared through this manuscript.

In the table of contents preceding the Introduction, you will notice that some of the chapters are unique to my work. I have received the teachings through daily communication and spiritual channels.

They are:

- *Consciously Connecting and Activating All 12 Chakras Of Our Body and The Auric Field.*
- *What Are The Benefits Of Sun and Moon For Humanity's Evolution?*
- *Ascension Of Love Consciousness To 'One Heart' 6D Consciousness*

Essentially, our expansive new reality and experience of the new realm are birthed when we are living through the heart moment to moment, in non-judgment. Our hidden might comes to life from abiding and operating through the heart center in all moments.

Consequently, the opening of the heart is pivotal to mastering a physical life and our form in the current high-frequency new realm. Therefore, the higher states of consciousness are possible only through the higher-self heart opened in action.

By exploring these basic facts in detail and learning the methods to master the new concept are adjusting our awareness to align with this monumental change in our reality.

Our frequency, by being aware in no judgment, through the heart in every moment, rapidly increases and alters our consciousness as needed for us to evolve day by day.

Once in this rapid acceleration state, we can catch glimpses of heightened awareness and our multidimensional being through the heart portal.

The fact is everything we need to evolve is already within us. Consequently, the focus is within and on developing our power within.

This manual contains wisdom and practices to assist the process of our unification within and with all that we are our original design and purpose in life.
Thus, we are fit for the outer world.

Table Of Contents:

Part One—The Principals Of The New Realm

Introduction

We are well into the New Era that started in August 2003. Additionally, we entered the Aquarian Millennium in 2020. The beginning of the Aquarian Age will allow full ushering of an idea and notion of the new era, which currently is taking off more powerfully.

The New Era has brought a higher frequency of light to Earth. Thus, allowing heighten awareness and the expansion of consciousness for humanity and all beings.

Consequently, the redirection of our experiences from solely mind-based onto the heart and soul-guided reality is critical for creating alignment and harmony within our present reality.

The opening of our hearts to love and compassion are necessary for success and our progress in this new paradigm.

Exactly, it is revival and awakening for most of humanity through the unification of our hearts, and the divine feminine with the minds, the divine masculine that we are mastering at this time.

This transfiguration of consciousness and awareness, based on heart-centered reality, brings forth our higher selves in purpose and a sink with the new earth.

The practice of living through the heart in the now sets us free from the limitations of mind consciousness grip and is when we settle in the creative flow of our original design.

Therefore, our manifestation powers can rocket through accessing and living our talents and abilities, through heart awareness moment to moment.

The Concept

Within this manuscript, we are relearning how to grow the light within our bodies, hearts, minds, and spirit. I shared the wisdom, knowledge, and practices pointing out to reclaiming the light within.

By removing blockages from and through our heart center, we connect and expand the eternal powers already within us.
Exactly, within our soul is the essence, the power for our evolution to the next levels of consciousness and awareness.

Consequently, this time is a grand unification of human accomplishments in the previous centuries and our mind's abilities with our unique eternal soul powers through the heart-portal of love and light within.

The manual is here to assist the evolution of our unification, through knowledge, recognition, healing, and opening the heart to its unlimited powers and eternal love and light we all carry within us.
With this love, we can bring our ascendancy through the gifts, abilities, and our unique frequency of light in co-creating the New Earth.

In this way, we can master the physical, and through sovereignty and integrity, experience our multidimensional limitless self and potential in every moment of living on Earth today.

In my anticipation that the awakening of the inner reality, realization journey and the flight through accessing the multidimensional reality happens gradually to every reader of this book, I included all the techniques and knowledge that I have used for this purpose.

The years of seeking and being guided by my higher self, and empowered by a few Spiritual Masters, made me content that the awakening to our higher potential and states of consciousness is possible and available to everyone, at this time.

It is my sincere desire to inspire and ignite the original flame and light, the source, and potential within many hearts.

The Manual For Humanity Thriving In The New Earth comes to life to make sure that no one is left behind on the path of awakening within.
Ultimately, to gather as many people to join forces in co-creating the new life and world on Earth, based on love, care, and cooperation

We all count in our new paradigm.
Let us begin.

In Love and Light,
Tat Jane

The Manual
For Humanity
Thriving
In The New Earth

Part One

The Principles Of The
New Realm

1

Our New Reality As A Consequence Of The New Model On Earth

With Mother Earth and all universes, we are evolving into the new stage of our collective and individual evolution. Humanity is moving into new levels of consciousness and awareness.

In this chapter, we will explore in more detail the wisdom and knowledge explaining the current changes in light frequency and their physical manifestations and sudden shifts we are presently experiencing on earth. Understanding and assimilating the concepts of rearrangements and alterations on earth will align us with what is so that we can benefit from these changes.

In other words, at this time, and just by not resisting and being one with what is, we can benefit the most.

The key is, as I mentioned in the introduction, that we transpose the focus and experiences to the inner world reality, within, through the heart, as opposed to focusing on the outside world and the mind's patterns. The current time is designed primarily for our rise and advancement within through the heart.

The chapter is to reveal this query and awaken what is not awake yet, in our consciousness and subconsciousness, when we can utilize our super-conscious experiences available to us at all times today.

Consequently, it will heal some wounds that were not able to heal and release under the influence of our busy mind, out of date programs, and grip. Our constant mind processing and struggles misaligned with the essence of the higher frequencies of light consciousness on earth, manifested for our expansion, need to let go of a grip.

When the mind is quiet, with no commends or chatter, it is allowing the time of revelations and our evolution to the next level.

For me, that has always seen mass consciousness expanding without limits, and in this human flourishing, this time is perfect bliss.

My vision can come to life at last.

To understand what I mean, let us go back in time, just a little bit.

After a partial Lunar Eclipse on Aug. 7th, 2017, and total Solar Eclipse on Aug. 21st, 2017, a new paradigm has dawned on earth.

The New Concept In The New Paradigm Is From Mind To Heart And Soul Power

Many are still wondering what is happening?
Things that are carefully calculated and programmed by our minds do not seem to work as they used to.

Despite many upheavals and destructions of kinds, the time is, frequency wise, perfect for us to rise within and to experience all we always wanted to be and to become.

How is this possible?

As mentioned, this is the significance of the new cycle, the Soul Light Era that began on August 8th, 2003, and took off globally, during the Summer 2018 Eclipse Season.

I will explain in the following chapters how the cycles of nature Sun and Moon influence and assist our human evolution far-reaching and globally.

Now, I would like to point out the difference between the Century and an Era.

The eras, there are three main eras, and they rotate, each lasting 15 000 years.

Exactly the eras are cycles of phases that the earth is going through. They are Universal, and they rotate, proximately every 15 000 years.

Three main eras are:

• **Far-Ancient, the** last Far-Ancient era started from about forty-five thousand years ago and lasted to about thirty thousand years ago.

• **Middle-Ancient,** the most recent Middle-Ancient era lasted from thirty thousand years ago to fifteen thousand years ago.

• **Near-Ancient,** the most immediate Near-Ancient era, where most of us were born in, also, we recently emerged from, started about fifteen thousand years ago and just ended in August of 2003.

4

When the new Far-Ancient era returned also, called the Soul Light Era, we are living now.

Consequently, the first 12-35 years is a transition period to the newly reincarnated Far-Ancient era, which is a reason of much turmoil, upheavals, and natural disasters on planet earth. Transition is inevitable and universal, and it is happening for all planets, stars, galaxies, and universes, also.

Despite the present turbulent reality on earth, in this era, as the name denotes, humans will have the opportunity to evolve on the Soul level, developing all kinds of personal talents and abilities to their full potential.

Additionally, the extraordinary abilities will be possible as a part of our soul evolution over the fifteen thousand years ahead.
The abilities such as flying, instant manifestation, and relocations without the use of a vehicle, to name a few, will be prevalent during and later in the present Far-Ancient era return.

Inevitably, and for our evolution's sake, the core difference between the new era and the one we just emerged from is that it is a soul-driven paradigm. The soul is taking over the mind, in all areas of our lives, from personal to the economy, politics, and all infrastructures is becoming the soul knowledge domain.

In other words, say good-by to old structures and looking on the outside for the answers. This cycle is about looking within and taking responsibility for creating our reality and birthing the new with our given resources, moment to moment, and in collaboration with our fellow man.

We all have to agree that this is a significant change, presently causing turbulence and dismantling of the old on all levels of our lives that are leading to the full unfolding of the new paradigm and our new reality.

Therefore, given that our old world is dissipating, a transposition of our experiences from an exclusively mind-based perspective to the involvement of the heart and soul experience helps our settling and progress in this new cycle.

I have written this manual to make this shift in our reality take place smoothly and naturally, given it is a critical reset for creating harmony and the opportunity to evolve in our lives on earth today.

Accordingly, our mind, body, and spirit need to assimilate and reset to the new constant, the soul, heart, mind, and body equation.
You can read that there is a heart in the new equation, because only through the heart, we can give the lead to our wise being within, the soul.

2

Heart Is The Core Of Life

The heart is the core of life because only by living through our heart experience of reality we can live our true selves and potential. Our true self is our higher self that comes to life when we live from our heart experience moment to moment.

When we are an expression of this higher-self love, we access the power to transform and heal our life. Our higher-self love is our greatest weapon and manifesto for success.

Looking back in time, maybe that was the reason for extensive manipulation, refocusing, and undermining of the power of owning the love within our hearts, including self-love, and towards others throughout the old paradigm.

In this era, the truth about the power of love for our human evolution and existence will be completely revealed, revised, and come to the forefront of our lives. The uprising of human awareness and mass awakening is closely related and determined with our ability to open our hearts to this love within.

All the challenges dissolve when we are an embodiment of the love within our hearts.

The truth is, all causes of human suffering are the lack of virtue. Yet, there is a virtue in everything. Love is a virtue. There is love in everything.

The very breath we take has so much virtue. The point is, we have to recognize, acknowledge, and appreciate it to thrive from it.

The new frequencies of light consciousness are helping with shifting our focus from being in our heads and trying hard to figure it out to consciously being aware in the now through the heart.
If for some this is not the case yet, please keep reading and taste it to experience the benefits.

When our point of reference comes from the heart center first, there is less room for confusion and feelings of lack and separation.

Time and distance do not exist when we feel this expansion of love from within. Consequently, our moral and ethics they shift too, suddenly we are part of everything. Thus, we feel empowered and centered, we are in higher states of consciousness.

Also, the new era is about our soul development. We need a pure heart to connect to our soul and align to its essence and needs. In other words, the pure open heart can hear messages and guidance from the wise being within, our Higher Self, the soul that are tailored for our acceleration path.
Why releasing the blockages from the heart matter the most?

Above all functions the heart has, it is also a bridge from the original message and the higher self--the soul, to the mind.

This wise, eternal, light being within, our soul, has all the wisdom for our transformation and acceleration, once we establish this connection through the heart center.
Therefore, one of the functions of the heart is to connect us to our essence, the original plan and message within.

So, the heart as a bridge to this expanded eternal knowledge within us has to be pure, without the pollution to support our evolution best.

Impurities are selfishness, greed, power-struggle, ego, and the attachments to outcomes, to name the few, stop the flow from within, and prevent the expansion of our consciousness and awareness.

The heart is also a receiver and transmitter of the information from the outer world and our original soul message to the mind.

That is why being present through the heart in every moment matters.

The mind's function is to process the information and call for action to direct the energy and matter-our body. When the mind receives a pure, heartfelt message through an open heart, it has no choice but to execute the most appropriate actions for our highest good and the good of all.

As we notice, involving our sincere heartfelt experience in the processing of the world today, and any time is crucial, and if our intentions are pure, can prevent unnecessary negative feelings and emotions concerning our reality.

In this manual, we are learning techniques to purify and open our hearts and establish this connection with our soul power. When in the sink with the powers already within us, we can experience our potential and evolve to higher levels of consciousness and awareness.

Additionally, when we purify our hearts and connect with our essence within, we experience liberation in our lives, and we are harbingers of freedom for others.

How to accomplish this?

At its core, being aware of our emotions, thoughts, and attachments and to consciously correct and redirect the energy through self-love, acceptance, and living from the heart, moment to moment is the place to start. As mentioned, self-love is critical for experiencing life fully, as well as necessary for evolving to the higher states of consciousness.

So, we first develop self-love and appreciation, to share the love with others.

Also, compassion, forgiveness, and gratitude for others and our lives are keys to this process of acceleration through the heart center.

With Mother Earth and countless planets, stars, galaxies, and universes, we are ascending and moving to the higher dimensions of consciousness where the lower frequency feelings, emotions, and states of mind, such as fear, worry, and separation cannot exist.

Therefore, we are responsible to clear the room, purify our soul, heart, and mind to evolve in this new reality. Where, living through the heart moment to moment align us within and with the outer world on autopilot.

On that note, I can see many people are still holding on guard in a state of self-protection. They believe if they were to operate from the heart, they are to lose control over things. That is an illusion and reminisces from outdated mind programs, not aligned with the New Earth and its parameters of high-frequency values.

Besides, lower frequency feelings, emotions, and not following our hearts' callings can create more blockages and prevents the natural flow of life and our evolution further.

Mother Earth already carries higher frequency and vibration for our expansion. So, being in the flow of our original design through the heart is essential for being in alignment within and with all things.

Therefore, the point is to surrender and allow available high frequencies of light on earth to carry out our evolution to the next levels, by living our truth, through the heart center, moment to moment.

Seeing Through The Heart–We Live The Truth of Our Being

When the heart starts beating life begins and when the heart stops life ends.
Likewise, when we are living our lives from the heart, we see and live the truth.
When we are solely led by the mind we get lost.

The heart is in the first place and the mind is on the second if you are looking to evolve and progress.
In other words, experiencing the life through the heart is the key for health, happiness, and acceleration in all aspects of life.

Why?

As noted, the Heart is a bridge to our true original design and purpose and the mind that produce the outcomes we live.

For this reason, staying focused in our hearts, at this time of significant shifts in frequency and other turbulence on our planet is rewarding.

When we are seeing the world through the heart, the picture is real and we live our truth.

Being In Divine Presence Through The Heart

Additionally, when we dwell in our hearts we are in the Divine, the Source presence, our higher self is the divine presence in our lives. The conditions of the Divine qualities such as unconditional love, forgiveness, compassion, care, harmony, and gratitude for our lives and others are within us.

Naturally, the same applies to the power that means the higher power for you, the cosmos, universe, galaxies, stars, Buddha, Bodhisattvas, saints, angels, and all ascended beings.

We are one with all things through our hearts.

Thus, we feel safe and protected and in the flow of our original light. Everything else seems to be unfolding in perfect harmony, grace, and ease.

Why?

Firstly, there is no separation within and with the outer world when we are living in the present moment through the heart.

Secondly, in this state of grace and harmony being present within, we can live our true passion. Our true calling and why we are here can spring forth. What is that we are meant to bring to this monumental time?

Connecting To Our Message Inside The Soul Temple

In Traditional Tao teachings, the space between the physical heart and Heart Chakra, in the middle of the chest, and a bit to the left, is called the Soul Temple (Ling Gong). Where within the light of our original–eternal soul resides the assigned message.

So, when conceived, we also receive a particular task to complete for that lifetime.

Consequently, it is significant to know about this sacred place and our Soul's message and task residing within the soul temple.

The practice and how to connect to the Soul Temple I explained in Chapter 20, Three Steps and Guidance To Overcome Challenges and Body's Soul Channel wisdom and practice.

The point is, in the light of this sacred space, in the middle of the chest, we can always find the strength to carry on, which is our task and intent. Therefore, through daily practices, we purify our hearts and establish a clear connection to the messages of our original design and purpose.

Essentially, clearing blockages, negative feelings and emotions, resistance, and attachments from our system and the heart is to be better vehicles of our original design, purpose and plan. Also, all the purification is primarily self-work.

Going back to observing oneself and consciously directing attention to the higher qualities existing within us and all things is the way to purify our channels for success.

Thus, being present in the moment through the heart is the golden key to recognizing our flaws, lack, and weaknesses that create blockages for our journey.

It comes down to taking responsibility in this new age and timeline.

Also, finding the light, and that which is good and accordingly reversing as otherwise.

Finding good within everything is the new team and the way to stop creating blockages for our evolution.

In other words, instead of being judgmental, we can be an observer and the healer, and what we can do to assist the situation. Finding the light in any circumstance or behavior, and seeing it through the eyes of love, forgiveness, and compassion is an opening for resolution.

By observing life through the heart's lens, we are less likely to accumulate negative information and blockages for our journey.

We Get To Choose Between Creating Blockages Or Accumulating Good Virtue

Our goal is to be co-creators and to birth the New Earth. The basic difference between the team and the course of action is to transform our consciousness and the consciousness of others by offering our Higher-Self virtues by living the truth through the heart.

It is time to be in a space of allowing things to unfold by creating a positive field, rather than controlling outcomes.

3

Physical Heart Vs. Spiritual Heart

U nderstanding our heart and its functions coalesce in assimilating our potential and abilities more fully. Also, to expand and utilize our gifts for the conscious shift in our awareness processing through the heart, which is necessary for our evolution, here is the information that will help and inspire.

Physical and Spiritual Heart is One.
The physical and spiritual heart is one firstly, because when the heart starts beating, life begins, and when the heart stops, life ends.
Here we are talking about our physical heart.

Likewise, in the second place, when we live from our hearts, we are living our potential while experiencing life in its true colors.
It is our spiritual heart that allows us to live in balance and harmony within and with the outer world.
When we do not live through our heart, our spiritual heart, we are missing out. Additionally, we can develop illnesses.

Our spiritual heart is the necessary counterpart, which creates balance, harmony, and peace within us and in our lives.

Often, people who suffer from heart and cardiovascular conditions, also other illnesses do not know and live this simple truth.

The Spiritual Heart creates the union we strive for that lies within us. The unity we seek is always available within us, and it was never on the outside.
We live the projection of our reality within. So, what we choose to perceive is the reality we also live.

When we live our lives involving the spiritual heart, we can create unity and oneness within us that is leading to harmony and peace with all things.

Living through the heart is quite an undertaking for most of the people today, and we will explore it from many different angles throughout this manual. Our goal is that by the end of the book, we are to be Masters of our form moment to moment through the heart.

Co-existence Of Physical & Spiritual In Everything

Let me explain further physical and spiritual existences within all things. They are one, and they operate successfully only as a unit.
It is one existence, containing two parts.

For instance, Yin and Yang are universal low because everything consists of yin and yang, as well as they subdivide endlessly. So, universally, the yin is the spiritual part, and the yang is the physical part.

The same is with masculine and feminine existence within all things.

Just like anything else, our heart contains the physical part, its function, the Yang existence, and its counterpart Yin existence.

16

Yin's existence concerning the heart, it is our spiritual heart, also known as Heart Chakra that is creating balance and harmony.

Therefore, understanding the essence of this universal law of Yin and Yang makes our lives smoother and more harmonious.

Firstly, we do not take things apart, but generally, we seek unity. harmony, balance, and union are the key to our health, well-being, and happiness. This is true, and the right way to examine our physical and spiritual hearts' purpose and significance.

Let The Heart Leads Your Physical Journey

For example:
Let us assume that you are walking, thinking, so many thoughts are on your mind. Something along these lines: oh, how I am going to do this, and I need that, and so on.

Then, suddenly your heart takes over, and everything instantly changes when ease and comfort replace the struggles of the mind.
In other words, you become one within, and with all that is on your mind. Instantly, your point of view has changed. Thus, you can come up with better solutions, simply because you have aligned and united with your spiritual counterpart, through the heart.

This example illustrates and points out that our spiritual heart is the heart of our life's journey.
Through our spiritual heart, we relate to others, our lives, and ourselves.

Spiritual Heart, also known as Heart Chakra, resides in the middle of the chest, and it mediates between the worlds of spirit and matter.

Both our physical and spiritual hearts are at the threshold of the realms of solid and tangible to intangible.

The Earth, water, and fire, which are the characteristics of the lower body parts and the physical world, are balancing with the intangibility of Air-- the upper body parts, the chest, throat, head, the chakras above the body, and the spirit world.

Through our spiritual heart, we balance these two realms that are in constant interaction. Thus, we harmonize our being within and with the outside world.

Additionally, through spiritual heart, we are evolving faster while practicing our divinity that thrives in forgiveness, compassion, and unconditional love.
Unfortunately, there are many people today that do not know and practice this wisdom of physical and spiritual heart co-existence, often having heart diseases, other illnesses, and health challenges.

Spiritual Heart the Symbol

Take a look at the symbol for the spiritual heart It is twelve lotus petals around six-pointed star

The archetype animal *associated with the spiritual heart is the antelope*

(two triangles overlapping). One triangle is pointing downwards, representing our spirit descending to meet the matter (body)– the physical world.

While the other triangle is pointing upwards, denotes the matter (our form) is rising to meet the spirit. So it is the balance of two worlds.

In Sanskrit, Anahata–the name for Heart Chakra, means 'unstruck' or 'sound made without two things striking' describing the co-existence of body and spirit in harmony.

The associated animal, the archetype is the antelope,

suggests someone in love. The wide-open eyes, restless wandering, and bounding with joy.

Let us explore this a little bit more.

When we experience life through our hearts, it is more likely that our minds will be harmonious, and at ease.

Why is this true? Even if we are not aware, the heart governs the mind. Furthermore, our heart is governed by our souls' desires and need.

All causes of our actions, experiences and our reality are initiated, and they come from our souls' message, through the heart. (Both, the physical heart and the spiritual heart)

The heart, especially our spiritual heart, is also a bridge between our spirit, its message, and the manifestation we live through mind-guided actions for most people today.
So, the mind receives the message and creates through actions the reality we live.

Therefore, our actions, our thoughts, and emotions, are primarily governed by our hearts and spirit, even if we are not aware of it.

Our Spiritual Heart Is Decision Maker

To recap, since it is significant to be aware of, it is not the mind that makes decisions in our lives.

For instance, when we experience the life, through the eyes of our spiritual heart, everything seems to be unfolding harmoniously. In other words, our spirit guides our motions. Our spirit is connected, and aligned, through our Spiritual heart, with our body.

Our message–our world within, is in harmony with the outside world, through our hearts.

To summarize, the heart's basic physical function is to keep us alive. **The second major heart's function is the ability and intelligence to guide our lives, in perfect harmony and ease.**

Follow Your Spirit Guidance

Being guided by our spirit does not desert us but heals and fortify our lives.
Our Spiritual heart carries a unique frequency and light of our spirit. Everything around us is a different frequency of light, and the highest frequency of this light is love.

Therefore, an unconditional love within our spirit is a powerful creator, instigator, and healer for our lives. The truth is when we activate and operate from this love within our spirit we are all-powerful architects and healers. It is just too difficult for many people to comprehend and believe in it.

One real cause of the challenges in our lives is the lack of our ability to recognize the virtue within everything, including the spirit within things.

Everything has a spirit and a virtue within. Try finding the spirit of love in everything to recognize this truth.

Consequently, realizing deep in our hearts the potential of experiencing love and the spirit within all things is a powerful fuel for our continuous acceleration.

4

The New Era--The Age Of Every Soul Light And Purpose

As we live through the first and the transition time of the New Era, named the Soul Light Era, what we need to be aware of while moving forward is a connection to our essence and the world within. Our soul is our essence, and this era is a soul-driven domain.

Thus, through this era and millennia ahead, all people will have the opportunity to develop their souls potential. Potential includes realization and manifestation of our unique soul abilities and virtues, especially once that benefit the collective and the areas of our lives and infrastructure.

As we can experience, the old world is collapsing and disintegrating from its roots, the new paradigm births in its place.

So, it is human evolution from within concerning the outside world and making a difference while building the New Earth and reality.

Inevitably, we will all be engaged to utilize our talents, wisdom, knowledge, and myriad of abilities to co-create this new world based on higher qualities and values of love, care, and co-operation.

Therefore, it is a perfect time for performing spiritual and energy practices to bring forth our hidden gifts, talents, and concepts to prepare and advance faster.

When we practice daily, and we implement conscious awareness through the heart center and connection with our inner world and powers from within, in stillness we learn to operate from our essence at all times.

As we know, the heart is connecting us to our soul purpose, where all the gifts are, and this is when we live our truth in action.

In conclusion, every aspect of our life flourishes when we connect and we are in alignment with our soul.

Why is this true?

To understand the point of this wisdom, let us review the characteristics of the soul.

The main characteristics of the soul:

~ Every thing and everyone has a soul.

~ Every Soul has consciousness and intelligence, which we can access through the heart.

~ Our Soul carries incredible wisdom, knowledge, and experience from our many lifetimes. Therefore, it is by far our best consoler and guide once we establish the connection, purify the heart, and trust with it.

~ The Soul can transmit its great wisdom and experience to the mind through our heart's portal.

~ Our Soul has a great memory

~ Flexibility

~ Communication power and abilities. The Soul communicates with other souls naturally.

~ Every soul has a certain healing power. The soul can self-heal and heal others.

~ Each soul can prevent sickness through its intuition.

~ Significant blessing capabilities when developed.

If you would like to experience this, when you are in difficulty, plainly ask your soul to bless your life. Your soul will find a way to assist you.

~ Incomprehensible potential powers when accessed and developed we exceed in all areas of life.

~ The Soul can protect and reward our lives.

~ Our Soul naturally follows spiritual principal and laws. Once we align with its flow and let go of the need to correct and adjust it, we experience our original powers and potential.

~ The soul is eternal and can reach enlightenment.

You can notice that all the above characteristics are accurate for every soul also, that they make every soul advanced and with limitless potential.

All we have to do is to initiate these characteristics and virtues by nurturing and continually be connected to our soul and to trust with it.

Therefore, by daily reflection and practice, we are establishing this connection and flow of our soul and its powers.

Consequently, the new era is also called the return of the Golden Age or Kingdom Age.

It is not hard to imagine that this is possible when all beings are connected to their essence and highest potential, purpose, and power through their hearts.

Additionally, everything has a soul. Our system, organs, cells, cell units, DNA, RNA, our health, business, relationships, and finances they have soul, too. So, it makes it easy for our healing and transformation process. By invoking and nurturing the soul of an issue, we are at the root of the cause.

I will explain the practical methods and implementation of the soul power for healing and transformation in the Practical Techniques chapters. In this chapter, we are exploring the essence of soul knowledge and how to utilize its wisdom in day-to day life.

The point is, when we connect to our essence, through realizations, energy practices, and meditation, we learn to evolve in every moment. These practices are not intended as a temporary state but ultimately, through expanding our consciousness, and inner intelligence to become the state of being.

There are two main practical techniques we can implement to support and speed up our evolution to the next level. They are energy practices and purification practices.

To perform energy practices is the way to transform our physical life and the form to a lighter and higher frequency version. In other words, through energy practices, we raise the frequency of our body, mind, and spirit. Thus, our all systems, cells, the smaller units, and all matter within become more vibrant and filled with light.

On the other hand, with purification practices and meditation, we remove blockages from our soul, heart, mind, and body to open the heart, again to increase our frequency and vibration. The more lighthearted, vibrant, and invigorated we are, the better life and performance we can generate. and attract.

Since, everything has a soul, as well as our systems, organs, cells, and the smallest matter also have souls, through energy and purification practice, we are increasing the frequency and vibration of all of them. So, both practical techniques are equally important.

They are part of the Yin and Yang universal principle, where energy practices are Yang and purification practices are Yin, which creates our physical and spiritual unification within.

So, we are refining our energy and frequency through different practices and techniques to increase our souls, heart, mind, and body frequency and potential and power.

Given that the highest frequency of light is love. Consequently, we are becoming embodiment of love and light.

Maybe it is new to some when we do spiritual practice and meditation; we are simultaneously healing and helping others grow and evolve, through our presence and on the soul level. Meanwhile by being love and light for all, we also accumulate a good virtue for our journey.

Therefore, our soul expansion is the expansion for many others too.

Through the energy, purification practices, and meditation, we firstly heal to transform, then we accelerate after we purify our hearts, souls, minds, and form more to enlighten them further.

As you notice, this is a lifelong task, and there are no limits in the amount of frequency and light we can hold.

The Benefits Of Connecting To The Essence Within

There are many benefits in being one with our soul—the essence within as the feelings of harmony and union permeate the heart, causing it to open further.

The soul has this perfection of love that passes all understanding once we unite with it, we can feel love take over our whole being. It is the feeling of coming home from a long journey.

Our spirit though is different. The spirit, we receive for this one lifetime, carries all the gifts and talents given to support our journey best. Often, for most people takes time for the spirit and the soul to merge as one, and it is when we live our highest destiny unified, here and now.

The spirit sometimes wants to live its way and until it realizes and learns enough to surrender to this unification with the soul that is necessary for the fulfillment of the original plan.

Also, the ultimate goal is to align our physical body and the life we live with our true-selves and our soul potential. So, this is all process of unification and fulfillment within that we are going through.

In Chapter 20, exercise 2, you can find the practice among others that helped me connect and establish the bond with my soul.

The next great benefit of this union within, which happens through practices, intention, and contemplation, is that the original light and passion are ignited, through the heart, when we experience this oneness of the form with spirit, is when our soul potential expands.

Additionally, when we are connected through the heart with our soul, the left and the right brain hemispheres are harmonized. When subconscious and conscious brains are in balance, we experience ease and comfort through everyday life and activities.

Through the balance and stillness of the mind, we gain soul intelligence and guidance from this wise, light, eternal being within. It is important to know while practicing, that all unfolds naturally, we do not need to plan or expect it to happen, all we do is surrender to the task at hand in love and gratitude.

I would imagine for everyone is a festivity to connect and unify with this eternal, enduring, wise, original, infinite being and source within.

Our practice and the path of discovery and realizations are continuing because the potential powers of every soul are endless.

Additionally, there are many layers of stillness and soul intelligence. For this reason, we continue to connect to the essence within, where all the love and wonder for our journey reside.

5

Grounding In Love And Gratitude For The Light Frequency Upgrade

G rounding in feelings of love and gratitude is vital at times of frequent and sudden events and the frequency of light changes on earth that we are experiencing now.

While the Earth and other planets are undergoing reconstruction and remodeling, so, us as humans and all beings are adapting to changes.

I am dedicating this chapter to the significance of grounding our energy and physical body within and with planet earth, helping us benefit from the new circumstances.

Allow me to introduce how grounding in love and gratitude and focus inward can regain our balance and sovereignty always and at times of upheavals.

Indeed, the Universe is blessing Mother Earth with the higher frequencies of light at all times during the ongoing transition time. We are in the ascension process, and planet earth frequency is accelerating. As we know, transfiguration is universal, and all planets, stars, galaxies, and universes are equally affected. For us, inhabitance, we are part of the alteration through our whole body and systems frequency and vibration changes.

In other words, our whole body is recalibrating to facilitate the higher frequency of light, including mental and emotional bodies.

Ultimately, these light frequency alterations and modifications lead to higher levels of consciousness and awareness for all.

Additionally, as we can witness, these frequency upgrades are remodeling our reality and social infrastructure while dissolving darkness and altering everything to their higher qualities and level of consciousness.

The ongoing reconstruction of our reality is manifested usually through sudden events and revelations.

Therefore when challenged, we need to focus and ground in the core of our body where our foundational energy is. Our main engine and powerhouse are in the lower abdomen, below the navel, and between 1st, 2nd, and 3rd Chakras.

Even just visualizing the golden sphere of light in this area can take off redundant pressure from our busy minds. Let me explain.

By consciously refocusing the energy and excess attention on thinking in our heads, we move it to where it is needed to boost our strength and power in the trunk.

Remember this wisdom, especially when you are in distress or disharmony to focus your attention to the light in the core of the body to boost strength within.

So, the grounding is necessary, especially when our physical body is undergoing transformations and frequency alterations, so as well is Mother Earth frequency accelerating and can assist our grounding.

The ongoing events are magnificent, and they are blessings for all beings, here on earth and beyond. Consequently, more people are awakening from slumber. Some are lead to become active contributors to this monumental time of change for all.

Others are slowly awakening.

Although frequency and light waves upgrades are happy events, they are also sudden and unpredictable. Their means are not revealed to people's awareness enough. Thus, they cause feelings of fear, despair, and unfortunate events throughout our society.
We have to feel compassion and empathy for those who struggle and to assist them when we can.

The best way to be beneficial to those around us, and our life, on these occasions is that we stay grounded in our foundation with love and gratitude.

How to do it?

We focus on the eternal forces within us, such as love, gratitude, and forgiveness for others and in our lives. In other words, it is our depuration and release of impurities from our systems that matter through these upheavals.

Knowing that and seeing everything taking place as an opportunity to evolve and go deeper within discovering our original intent here and now is rewarding.

The feelings of love and gratitude can fortify the momentum. We connect to the state of deep appreciation and love for all we have and have ever had focused in our foundation.

The point to know and be aware and swift is as follows:

Whenever frequencies on our planet, which is an ongoing event, are changing and becoming higher, simultaneously, all of us living beings are receiving an upgrade in our frequency. For this reason, while and before we are affected and transfiguring in our physical, mental, emotional, and spiritual bodies.

Being aware that these shifts are happening and not to take them lightly, we are attuned and grounded in our foundation to prevent possible unfortunate events that often take place at the same time.

By shifting the focus from external to internal and sharpen our awareness and attention to within us, as opposed to the outside world, can help us.

Also, knowing that our thoughts and emotions are critical to our actions and experience. Checking out what messages we are sending out to our field of energy can help too.

In other words, we are mastering our physical, mental, emotional, and spiritual aspects through these upheavals and our unification within unknown and unpredictable circumstances as they occur.

One negative thought, if not addressed in love, forgiveness, gratitude, and light, at these times of turmoil, can attract a lot more negative energies coming our way. So, we pay more attention. This is the awareness and being present in the moment-to-moment, through the heart center that we are mastering to evolve. These events are planned for our evolution through the purification process.

Consequently, we are not allowing any space and any chance for dark messages and dark energies to prevail and take over our mental, emotional, spiritual, and physical bodies.
What do we do?

So, when we recognize that some negative message comes up from the outside world, or in our thoughts or feelings that may arise within, we have to acknowledge them and not push them away.

I suggest looking into these negative disturbances, sincerely and deeply. When we observe our behavior from this perspective, through our hearts in reflection, we can realize the root cause of their appearances more easily.

Depending on how attuned we are, often we can see or feel what causes disharmony within us immediately. Know that even if you do not realize why something is manifesting in your life, it is the same, what we are to do is send the loving thoughts back.

By offering forgiveness, appreciation, and being thankful for the troubling event, the person, the thought, or emotion in due course will heal.

We may see or feel an immediate relief in our bodies, overall feeling towards the occasion.
On the other hand, when blockages or negative memories are too deep within us, they can come back. In other words, they need more love and forgiveness to heal. The key is not to be irritated by them coming back. Instead, we repeat the process of healing these wounds with our love, forgiveness, compassion, and being grateful while focused on our foundation, until they convert. Usually, these intense feelings take up a lot of energy so, what we can do to help is repeat the following affirmations, silently or aloud, for a minimum of three times each:

"I call light to this time and space, now!"
Visualize the light from the universe and Mother Earth satiating the room or space all around you.

"I call the golden rain shower to wash away my aura, now".
See the golden shower washing all negative information from your system.

"All the energies I have given away and I left behind, return to me, now".

Feel all the energy you have spent uselessly in the past, coming back to you.

In conclusion, grounding our physical, mental, emotional, and spiritual bodies in our core and feelings of love and appreciation can assist our journey always, especially at challenging times. Thus, we are managing our awareness of the inner world of thoughts and emotions to master them. So, that nothing outside of us can impact our awareness that is in our foundation and feelings of love and gratitude.

When we are well-grounded, balanced and resilient, in our trunk, we emit the waves of harmony and are less likely to attract negative experiences. As the vehicles of everlasting love and gratitude within our hearts and body via the trunk, we are the ambassadors of light and fortitude.

Please refer to Part Two, Practical Techniques, Chapter 21 for more wisdom and practice on creating a strong foundation.

6

Living Eternal Now Moment Through the Heart

I n relearning being in the now moment as the part of the winning model, for our acceleration in the new reality, have you experienced the eternal now moment?

If you have not, move your focus to your heart that will help you to be fully present in the now.

When we experience a present moment through the frequency of our hearts, we hold the vibration of love and we can actively live in union with our infinite self. In essence, through the heart center, the sphere of light in the middle of the chest, we access the capacity of love that is eternal. Our soul is eternal, thus, through the heart in the now we can experience our soul's eternal heart and eternity.

What is the significance?

The significance is the expansion of our consciousness and entering the path of true awareness, and awakening in the present moment. Consequently, we avoid unnecessary struggles of the mind's desire to control and change the things and circumstances.

Instead, we hold the vibration of love and abundance in than flow of our original design and its main purpose to evolve. Our hearts fully present in the now through this love thrive from the higher frequencies of the new earth and our new reality.

We are in the ascension and acceleration process with Mother Earth, and all other planets and beings throughout the cosmos and galaxies. One can ascend only in harmony and alignment within and with the outside world, through becoming the embodiment of love through the heart in the now.

Anyone that has no love for others and self will not ascent to the new realms of consciousness at this time.

Therefore, the first is the unification of soul, heart, mind, and body through the frequency of the heart in the now.

When we are fully present in the ever-present now and the perfection of love in our hearts, we experience the unification within.

Why is this more possible today than ever before allow me to explain once again.

In the twentieth century and centuries before, mind over matter played a vital role in human lives and our evolution. Human has developed tremendously through our minds abilities. It is remarkable to know, that with the 21 Century, as I mentioned earlier, since August of 2003 the New Era has begun.

In this era, the soul will play a vital role in human evolution and all aspects of our lives.

Consequently, it is beneficial for us to align within and to be connected to our soul and its power. The only way we can be in alignment with our soul at all times is when we are attuned within, through the heart, in the now.

Attention within through the heart is the shift that creates the different dimensions in our new realm and reality..

Naturally, the new concept requires some effort and for us getting used to operating through the heart perceptions and expressions. But once we experience the expansion of consciousness and liberation by being fully present in the now through the heart, we can grasp the significance of this new model designed for our evolution.

Also, frequent changes and higher frequencies of light on the new earth make living through the heart in the now natural. In other words, at this time to benefit, we perceive through our hearts' eyes to align within and with the outer world.

Consequently, we are in the sink and not going against the stream while living our lives and day to day activities in these new settings and reality. We are becoming more sensuous, flexible, and inventive, thus more aware with what is at the moment.

Additionally, we can avoid confusion and the issues caused by overthinking through our minds' old set patterns, how things should be or look like, and so on. Instead we are observing through our hearts, doing what we can, trusting, and believing in this new concept for our evolution. Always know, if negative thoughts, feelings or emotions start accumulating, you have left the present moment and the heart experience. Just come back gently to the now that is always perfect.

Of course, we use all the knowledge our mind has but more like a flight since the cause of our actions and the processing derive from the heart experience.

Where crux is to be attuned and present, guided by our heart and soul potential and purpose in every moment.

Through current circumstances, events, and our new reality constructed moment to moment, people are realizing that kingdom within is the way to liberation. This also makes focus inward in the now a global shift.

The New Reality In The Ever New
Now Moment

So, at this significant time of rapid higher frequency of light consciousness that is dissipating density within us and our reality, it is a new beginning with every now moment.

Once we emerge in the now, through the frequency of our hearts, we are aware that everything reflects the purity of our hearts and souls at that moment.
Consequently, we are the sovereigns through this love and power within where every moment can feel infinite and eternal. When we let the now moment through our hearts lead the way, we experience the flow and ease. So enticing as nothing else exists.

In delight, I remember reading the books on being in the NOW, decades ago. It seemed a great idea although I was not able to actualize it, due to my busy mind always wanting to change and adjust something about the moments in time.
Today, I can see clearly how futile that was, also how futile this is for many people even today. We can never change the outside world. We can only change the world within us to attract different circumstances. I can see it today, I was missing the point that was and is, the now moment through the heart experience is the key.

Please make a note that being fully present in the now in your head, through thought patterns and emotions, preprograms guided by the mind, nowadays is more dangerous than ever. Because of more turmoil than ever thus, the key is to be fully present through the heart in the now for our expansion and liberation at this present time and always. This is when we see our reality through the love and compassion of our hearts, regardless of what outside reality is.

Here, we are going a step further learning and mastering how to change our frequency and message, to become the magnet for our acceleration journey through the heart.

Besides, it is so easy to let go and let the heart lead the way, today. The fact is the crisp high frequencies of the new earth keep us anchored in the present, and our presence in the now effortlessly. All we need to do is be in our hearts to experience it.

Being On The Acceleration Path At All Times, We Lock In The Now

Not all the moments are enchanting, but a comfort zone is not where we accelerate. It is when we feel uncomfortable that we learn the most about others, our lives, and ourselves. So, letting the moment teach us, by being aware of its message through the heart's experience, is being on the acceleration path at all times.

Through our heart's eyes in the now, we see the truth and are less prone to manipulation and confusion from the outer world, too.

When it feels uncomfortable, and until we adjust, the key is to endure the moment again through the heart in trust. There is always something positive about all occasions. So, we focus within through the heart to learn what is a moment to reveal to us.

When we are in the now and processing life through the heart in trust, the fears and doubts can hardly overcome the experience.

Tune Into The Eternal Now Through Your Heart

Tune inward.

Feel the love, the comfort, and greatness when the heart takes over the moment.

Because the heart in the now connects us to our eternal soul message and purpose there is no need for a rush. One cannot achieve anything by pushing and rushing through to it. Now, to tune in and feel the moment, through the heart first, it is becoming the manner of the time.

Inevitably, a saying, to be at the right place at the right time is changed to being present within in the now through the heart and to trust, it is the right place to be.

Wondering do you also feel that glorifying the past and making many plans for the future has lost its grip in our New Reality. These mind patterns are rarely an option today.

Fortunately, the new era brought the new concept that consists of nothing to linger on and to hope for; it is all here and now.

So, not to dwell on the past, and think about what the future may bring, is an important step forward in our evolution.

It is about the truth and taking responsibility through the heart in the now. Thus, the next now moment is a product from this now.

Everything is possible and depends on the frequencies we are vibrating and emitting at the present. Therefore, be content through the heart experience moment to moment to thrive and evolve in this new realm and reality.

Harmony And Unity In The Now

Only through the heart, we can experience harmony and unity with all and what is.

Our hearts know what we need and what is best for us to experience the next.

Therefore, by surrendering to the present moment in harmony, not trying to change something, we are allowing our hearts and souls to flow our experiences in grace and ease.

It is liberating, and our pure essence to allow the heart at all moments to lead the way.

When we are one with the Now, in this perfect love within, we are the source and the master of our reality.

The Unfolding Of The Grand Plan In The Now, Moment-To-Moment

Have you experienced the phenomenon of being fully present in the now moment through the heart before? If not, it is the perfect time to relax into it from today.

Imagine all humanity as one in the now, in love and gratitude through our hearts, what kind of power would be available on earth and everyone.

Not only in my vision, being one with now through the heart is the grand plan for the New Earth and the full realization of the higher realms of consciousness and awareness on our planet.

Until the grand vision unfolds, we keep up by being in the present moment through our hearts, in love, gratitude, and service.

7

Celebrating Birth And Rebirth In Every Now Moment

C elebrating birth and re-birth in every now moment through our hearts, and breath.

Our heart breath is an ever-present light-force and energy of the universe through us.

With every conscious heart breath, we connect to grounds of source within us.

We all have the source within us, our original light-source that we are one breath away. This Phoenix within is ever seeking and ready to reinvent itself.

Those who believe in themselves and others, living fully in the now through the heart, are reborn by virtue itself within every moment.

Specifically, there is a virtue in everything; we can choose to thrive from it.

When we stay in this zone of projecting ourselves and others for the highest good, we emanate the source of nourishment to all.

To be specific, we can choose to nurture our surroundings and self by merit of living in purpose, harmony, and peace within.

The Birthing Of An Idea, Kicks Open The Journey And Our Evolution

Growing up, I thought that the middle of the road is a good place to be. I remember that 'Golden middle' was always my choice.

Turned out that the middle of the road, in real life, does not exist.

Sincerely, I wanted to connect and to be part of all things.

Lately, by meditating on One Heart consciousness, I realized that the seed of 'one heart' was dawning within me at this young age.

Eventually, I had to take part in something.
Early on, I chose to stand for the Light.
It was the birthing of an idea that kicked open my journey in pursuit of light forces in life.
Once I realized that my idea created an opening to the whole new world of new beginnings and closures, the journey has begun.

One thing is certain we have to have a firm notion for something we believe in and after to continue to ride upon it.

Once I found my persuasion, it was evident to me that when we finalize and learn from a sequence in life, we can move on to the next level.
So, early on, I have made peace and a deep connection with the inevitable process of rebirth and reinvention through concluding and starting over.

To this day, I owe much love and gratitude to the novel 'Demian' by Herman Hesse.

The following paragraph impacted me the most:

"The bird fights its way out of the egg. The egg is the world. Who would be born must first destroy a world. The bird flies to God. God's name is Abraxas."
Herman Hesse

Abraxas is the ancient God--the myth claimed to be both God and the demon. Also, represents the way to true origin.

Among several meanings of this paragraph, the wisdom is also:

Once we receive the knowledge and what we need for our evolution, the old world vanishes.
Also, polarities meet, and they are part of the whole.

Good and evil, life and death, the truth and lies, light and darkness exist at the same time in all circumstances of life that lead us to our origin.

Additionally, we have all the shades in-between for our navigation.

Indeed, either part or all the shades in between are meaningful.
The knowingness of birth and rebirth we once take upon, through our hearts, with no fear, and with trust, can move our journey fast.

Sometimes for our best interest and evolution, we have to have the heart to close or terminate things.
We can find the strength in knowing that by doing so, we are opening the door for the new to come.

The new is the progress, even if sometimes does not look that way. In other words, it is right to believe that all that unfolds in our lives is for our best interest and to reflect on why something happens for the best. Spending time in retrospection is rewarding while we create our destiny by processing and adapting our nature through the occasions we live.

Every moment is an opportunity for the birthing of the new idea, and another step to take for moving forward in our pursuit. Therefore, the ending up is the new beginning on the horizon. And then, there is love. Love is such an inspiration in our lives.

Stay in your heart dear souls, to feel the love in every now moment.

Negative Memories Serve The Birth And Rebirth and Our Evolution

Speaking of a closure, there are times when negative memories come to teach us lessons. They also tend to keep us in one place for sometime and until we receive all the knowledge needed for the next chapter of our life.

Life is like a school program, where we get the opportunity to learn and pass the exam, to move to the next level.

So, through all the occasions, reflecting through our hearts, focused on the best we can do in a moment, and trust in devotion is an optimal concept.

The new earth and our new reality are based on this optimal concept.

Therefore, our destination is the journey, where we get to purify and create virtue, an opportunity for people around us and our life.

I believe the goal of one's life is the unification within and with the outer world through becoming one with eternal love and light of our heart and soul.

That is why birth and rebirth are vital for our purification process and becoming the light and one with the eternal love of our hearts and souls moment to moment.

When we choose to be the source of love and light, everything in our lives reflects in the same way. With our purpose, and as the resource of this love our evolution journey is a path of acceleration in a pure bliss for all.

Soul Wisdom Vs. Mind Knowledge

It is when we doubt and complain about the process we lose the ground.

Often our mind is inclined to process through the old memories, and the ways we have experienced something before.

So another fact is, what is in our consciousness already, it is not helpful at the times of our evolution to the next level of our lives.
Why is this true?
Everything that is in our consciousness is the level we are at.

For this reason, in the event of our intense evolution to the next level, we seek knowledge from our souls' through the heart.
As many times noted, our soul has wisdom, knowledge, the experiences, from many lifetimes that can create the depth and more meaning of the experiences we live.
A rule of thumb is looking beyond the surface to seeing and knowing the essence of things. We can accomplish seeing and realizing the essence of something by being one with the moment through our hearts.

Forgiveness Practice Can Open Our Hearts For The Rebirth And Speeds Up Our Evolution

Practicing forgiveness is helpful at times when we need to move to the next level and we have the emotional, mental, and other residues from the previous chapter in life. Forgiveness is a great way to resolve the old by going deeper in sincerity and recollection, releasing negative memories and attachments to already known.

Thus, forgiving our self and others helps the opening of the heart to the process of death, rebirth, and evolution further. Consequently, forgiveness practice facilitates a conclusion of one cycle in life and the birthing of the new, through a smooth transition.

In Chapter 18, I explained Forgiveness practice wisdom in detail and how to practice forgiveness to speed up our evolution.

8

Inspiration And Motivation Equal Self-Realization

On The Self-Realization Path, It Is The Inspiration And Motivation That Matter

D o you agree that on the path of self-realization, inspiration and motivation are the fuel, which keeps us going?

In this chapter, I will explore with you, what it takes to be inspired, motivated, and remain on the self-realization journey infinitely.

It is surely, the way to be forever young and free, self-content, and to be in good spirits.

I hope my realizations for the inspiration, and motivation on our lives' journeys to self-realization, inspires you. I wish to ignite the light within your hearts, too.

This flame within, once ignited, can unmistakably remove possible boundaries that often stand in the way of a great, free, flowing of our creative energies and manifestation powers.

It is equally important that our innate need to be of

assistance and to contribute to the world is ignited and set free.

I carry in my heart an everlasting desire to expand my consciousness and the consciousness of others.
To be exact, it is my burning desire to liberate and expand the horizons for others and my own.
This internal drive keeps me inspired and motivated at all times, therefore, it is been an enchanting journey to pursue.

What I discovered is that the ultimate truth of our being is our self-realization path.
More precisely, the self-realization is plural, since we are on an ongoing journey of self-realization through a myriad of self-realization.
It is an ongoing process of becoming self-realized through many self-realizations of our original light and message within.

The Flame Within Is An Everlasting Inspiration

What is that which lights the flame within your heart? For everyone the flame is different but a few characteristics are the same for all.

Firstly, it is something that motivates us, to go the extra mile, even when nothing seems to be going our way. When we go the extra mile, we ultimately forget about temporary things, and ourselves then we are one with eternity.
Eternity is the flame within our hearts.
Therefore, it is the place where we can always find the strength and fuel to keep us moving on.
So, the flame within our hearts is our anchor point and we are well on the fast track to self-realization.

Secondly, the flame ignites unconditional love within us.

When our hearts are ignited and wide open, in this unconditional state, we can flow out our higher selves' in purpose.

For this reason, on the path of self-realization, the wholehearted journey is the point and the magic, not the destination.

The destination is a motive, an idea, in our hearts, but it is the journey that counts and brings rewards for our evolution.

Thirdly, the flame within us is an everlasting well of the ideas for the next stepping-stone to stepping on. In other words, it is a generator of the inspirations and motivations on our journey to self-realization.

Understanding Our Original Message--The Flame

It is the flame, which is the consciousness and the message that inhabits the body when one is conceived.

So, we have come to a physical form and at this special time with a particular purpose to fulfill.

The sooner that we can connect with our original intent and start realizing this highest plan, the sooner we can be on the self-realization journey.

When we look sincerely, since we came to this physical world, all we want is a feeling of unity, harmony, and wholeness within and with all that is.

Since our kingdom is within us, I suggest looking within for the answers, and on the outside for the ideas to reflect upon.

Although we are all One and part of the grand field, we are all the source seed and our unique message.

The message, the flame within us carries all the inspirations and the motivations we will ever need on our self-realization journeys.

All our gifts, abilities, talents, and all abundance of possibilities are within our hearts and souls.

We carry our unique light frequency and message. Also, we are part of the frequency, and light of everyone and everything, all things through our hearts.

Consequently, we are entirely connected and part of this gigantic quantum entanglement and field.

Now, all we need to do is be aware of our thoughts, we are literary creating and living the results of our thoughts.

Thus, expanding the consciousness and awareness through the heart, reaching out through this center, to the field and as many people as we can is being in the timeless universe of creation.

This is also, the quickest way to self-realization, being an active participant in the quantum field of creation.

As a result, we become the vehicles and benefactors to the lives of others and our lives.

In the context of the quantum field of creation, there is no separation. The separation is an imaginary concept of the old paradigm, which was based on dependence and manipulation.

The New Earth and the true Divine, the Source desire for all beings is the unification of soul, heart, mind, and body and the unity and one heart consciousness for all.

The unification of the physical form in the unity of the heart consciousness and awareness is the grand plan for living in the new earth and era.

So it is a perfect time to activate the flame and our message within and start realizing our true potential, through actions and deeds. On the self-realization path with faith and self-esteem, through love, we can discover and live our flame infinitely.

Connect To The Original Flame
And The Massage

So we know we have the source within us, our source and message, which can easily surface when we are fully present in the now.

Our ultimate goal is to be the masters of our destiny, and our heart is the key.

The heart is a connection between our true, original soul messages, in this case, the flame, to the mind that organizes actions.

In other words, our body is directed by our mind's energy. Although, this force derives from our soul messages, through the flame in our heart directing the mind, which moves the matter and creates the outcomes we experience.

This is why we have to have the flame lit up at all times to be the source of our inspiration and everlasting motivation on our path to self-realization.

The Key To Self-Realization Is The
Awakening Of The Flame Within

To live our true hearts' desires and our soul's purpose we need to:

First, we have to connect and recognize the flame within our hearts. What it is and to discover the original plan for our life.

We open our hearts and listen without attachment to the outcome.

Second, we already know, we need to purify our hearts from the possible preconceptions and attachments to the outcome, which is hearing and believing only what the mind can conceive.

Use your heart's ability to expand your consciousness and to allow the receiving of authentic, clear messages from your soul.

In this way, our manifestations, on the journey to self-realization, are aligned with our true hearts' and souls' desires and needs. At the same time, we are in the free flow of our creative energies; we are inspired and motivated by being guided from the source and the flame within.

Examples Of The Questions To Ask On The Path To Self-Realization

The idea is to connect to our original flame within, every day. For a few minutes in the morning when our minds and our preprogrammed concepts are not fully awake, it is a good time to ask questions and seek guidance from our Higher-Self and the soul.

For instance, we can ask:

A. How can I ignite the true passion, the flame within my heart, to assist my self-realization journey?

B. What is the next step I can take that can take me closer to living and realizing my true calling?

C. Is there anything I need to know today so that I can be more effective on my self-realization journey?

Be creative and imaginative, have the questions with the specifics that reflect your self-realization path.

The Highest Purpose For Most People' Is To Be Of Service To Others

When we think sincerely, the highest purpose of our lives is to be a vehicle to others, too. Indeed, the self-realization path is a path of service to others also, that when we do we feel energized and fulfilled.

One of the greatest services, which happen to be a great inspiration and motivation, is to offer love and receive love. Similarly, to offer and receive the love through different acts of service is the highest achievement.

Whether we are on the self-realization path through any act of contribution such as writing, teaching, tailoring, construction, singing, or driving a vehicle, it comes down to giving and receiving love through a particular service and making a difference.

When we come to a realization and the potential of being of service while thriving through our flame that is love and passion within, we are already halfway done.
Now, we just have to connect to this flame within when our hearts are wide open, inspired, and to be in pursuit.

If we are not sure what the destination is, on our self-realization path, we can visualize it not as a place but rather the field of energy we are moving towards.
When on the right path that leads to self-realization, we feel energized and motivated.

The good sign that we are on the right path is that our hearts open, rather than contract.
We are in the flow, just like a straw in the river, where we do not need to try hard to navigate. Also, another good sign is, we feel as we are part of and we can prosper.

If it feels hard for some time, and our energy is draining, we are probably not in alignment with our flame, purpose, and plan. It is a good signal for us to reflect on why and to change the course slightly.

I believe that the physical life we choose is to be of service and in alignment with our original true flame and plan. The flame within is to be lit up and thrive in harmony through all phases of the self-realization journey. Therefore, it is clear to realize when we are off the course and when the path becomes a struggle.

Once on the right path that leads to self-realization, it is a blessing, we are energized, nourished, motivated, and inspired. This is when our soul power grows and we are receiving good virtue.
Good virtue is the spiritual currency for our good deeds, which is food for the soul, and everyone around us is being nurtured.

The point is here:

If our creation finds even just one person and inspires and motivates their self-realization journey, we have succeeded. Moreover, we helped the overall frequency of our collective, we help our planet to accelerate further, and more people to be inspired and be the contributors, and on the self-realization path.

.

9

Conscious Breath To Heightened Awareness

To connect within nowadays it is easier than ever before, we are supported by the current higher frequencies of light on Earth. I found that conscious breathing is effective in experiencing heightened awareness, inner peace, and contentment.

In this chapter, I will explore with you the conscious breath and breathing as a vehicle to accelerate faster on our journeys always, and at this time especially.

The breathing techniques I will introduce can shift us easily to higher levels of consciousness and awareness. Entering these states we can experience a perfect bliss within and with the outside world.

Let us begin.

The idea is to focus on each breath through the heart, since it can assist us in entering a full awareness in the now that by design and steadily unfolds into heightened states of consciousness.

Exactly, I am entering the state of a so-called perfect bliss through my conscious breathing through the heart at any moment. So, you can do it also, try it today after reading on how in this chapter.

Let me explain further, why letting go and focusing on

the breath can expand our consciousness and support the experience of heightened awareness.

The Power Of Now Through The Conscious Breath And Breathing

I have realized that the conscious experience of each breath brings more power to the present moment, and at the same time, it ignites the feeling of true belonging to the here and now.
I found that belonging to hear and now is ecstatic and it moves our lives in more perfect harmony and flows from within.

Moreover while practicing, we can experience belonging beyond this time and space. The feeling of belonging beyond time and space is eternal; as a result, we can catch glimpses of eternity a higher state of consciousness, here and now.

In delight it dawns to me, we have spent quite some time reading and learning about different levels and state of consciousness and the time has come to experience it on Earth, naturally today.
I am referring to the state of consciousness, also know as the Samadhi or a Perfect Bliss state, we can obtain through conscious breathing with some practice.

Through these occurrences, I am certain we do not need to go to the caves of the Himalaya Mountains, to experience the benefits of conscious breathing techniques. We can live their full power, right here and now, wherever we are on Mother Earth.

To illustrate further, I feel my every breath like a soft pillow between the experience of my physicality and all creation, including all animate and inanimate beings.

I brushed on Tantric ancient yogic breathing techniques for our faster acceleration.
The Yogic breathing comes to my mind on the lake, one day.

I had an aha moment, followed by the variation of the same technique while walking and focusing on doing this ancient technique.
Exactly, I have been guided to practice this breathing since one of the Tidal Waves of Light frequencies that often grace the earth at this time.
These waves of light brush the earth, removing darkness and increase our ability to access the altered states of consciousness more easily.
It will be more tidal waves of higher frequencies of light in the years to come until the transition is completed.
Luckily, we are evolving, together with Mother Earth and other planets, accelerating to higher levels of consciousness and awareness.

So, I feel like I started learning to breathe again by paying attention to each breath I take while walking or doing other activities. In the most extreme ways, like the ancient yogis, and through the new frequencies of light on the earth, we can reach heighten awareness through breath and breathing.

Take a deep breath and intentionally pull in all the light frequencies available into your body. Feel and see the breath expanding and relaxing all the cells, systems, organs, they are receiving nourishment from the Universe and the earth below. Gently exhale and feel the cells contracting now by releasing any tension and impurities. Feel yourself surrendering and becoming one with the vastness of the Universe.

Visualize your central channel and all the chakras connected, in a brilliant white column of light. Continue nourishing and invigorating yourself for a few minutes by drawing-in more air and the light-frequencies of the Universe above and the crystal core of the Earth below.

With each conscious breath, we can raise our frequency higher and towards the frequency of those celestial beings. Just by doing a couple of rounds of breath, in and out, and by visualizing the high light-frequencies coming through us, we feel invigorated, peaceful, and inspired for our day.

Performing any of the breathing techniques from Chapter 22, Part Two of this manual is a powerful way to increase our awareness in the now, expand the consciousness by oxygenating with the current higher frequencies of light available when in nature or indoors.

Have in mind, we can breathe the light and energy force of the universe into any of our momentary challenges and see/feel their frequency transforming to light frequencies and dissipating into the eternal flow of the Universe.

You can experience moving the light and the light force of the Universe through the Heart or any organ, systems you choose in the same way through being fully present, conscious breathing, and visualization.

Observing ourselves and being aware of the breath and the light is the key to awakening and being on the heightened awareness path.
Thus, taking a conscious breath through the heart and observing the world through the eyes of love, performs miracles on a path of mastering awareness and our acceleration to the higher states of consciousness.

10

Consciously Activating And Opening Chakras In Our Auric Field

Human Auric Field–The Chakras Outside Of The Body

Our physical body is our best vehicle for this realm on Earth. Although at times we feel confined within it. Therefore by implementing energy and meditation practices, we are transforming the dense matter within our body into lighter and higher frequency form.

Besides, in the following chapters, we will learn how to expand our consciousness and awareness beyond just the physical realm and to connect to the infinite and the source of all creation.

One of the ways to expand beyond the physical, and what we can see, is to connect to the Chakras that are outside of our form and in the auric field.

Again, through conscious breath, we can bring in Prana- the energy and light force of the universe to the

Chakras in our auric field. Doing so, we increase the body's frequency and vibration; expand our consciousness and our energy field.

I am aware most of the readers are familiar with the Seven Chakras within our bodies but are less familiar with the significance of the six additional energy vortexes that belong to our auric field and are outside of the body.

The zero or the Earth Star chakra is 3' below the feet rooted in the ground, and five more chakras are above the head. They all create our aura and the energy field that we are constantly vibrating and emitting out to the world through our frequency.

Our energy body and our body's auric field attract all that we experience in our lives. So, by connecting this energy field around us with the physical body, and working to clear it of blockages, we are more likely to attract what is in harmony and alignment with our true nature and purpose. Consequently, on the physical, mental, emotional, and spiritual levels, we feel unified, uplifted, and divinely guided through our lives.

In the following paragraphs, I will point out the main characteristics of these Chakras in our auric fields that are critical to our growth and acceleration path. In the chapter that follows, we will consciously connect them with our physical bodies.

Chakra 0~Is The Earth Star Chakra

Earth Star chakra is our personal, unique connection to the Earth's life force and the crystal core in the center of the Earth. As you may experience, the Ultimate Creator's Light exists within the core of the Earth.

So, when you begin your meditations you can start with sending a grounding cord of light from your belly button to the source within the earth. The grounding allows us to experience the higher dimension of consciousness more easily while activating the rest of the energy vortexes outside of our physical forms

The chakras above our heads are:

The 8th Chakra Is The Soul Star Chakra

The Soul Star Chakra is located six inches above the 7th-Crown Chakra on the top of the head. When this chakra is opened and activated, the Creators Light can flow through this energy vortex of light above our head, freely, allowing us to access higher states of consciousness.

Consequently, we experience the highest Love from the Divine, the Source, and other Ascended Masters, which allows awareness of our ultimate powers as Spiritual beings.

Our Soul Star Chakras is a vessel of our eternal Soul's energy and contains the essence and power of our accumulated soul experiences throughout many lifetimes.

When we can, through meditation and practice, dwell in this realm of the 8th--Soul Star chakra, we can experience more of our souls' abilities. Simultaneously, we can communicate with the Ascended Masters that are aligned with our intent here on earth at this time.

When fully activated, open, and as a result of one's total soul realization, purity, and devotion the Akashic records wisdom and data are available and possible within the Soul Star Chakra.

The 9th Chakra Is The Spirit Chakra

The Spirit Chakra is the vortex of energy and spirit we received for this life. When open and activated our Spirit vortex of energy and vibration will enable us to connect to potential power of our spirit, then after to the vast realm of spirit. Here, we realize and establish our direct connection with the Source.

Therefore, we can communicate with light beings from around the galaxy, angels, guides, and star beings.

When this energy center is fully open and activated we are completely surrendered to the Flow of our Spirit, allowing the Divine, the Source will to flow and guide our experiences. This chakra is the gateway to access our Soul's gifts and abilities to the full extent and to be free to share them with the world.

Our direct connection to the Source allows us to experience, draw upon, and realize our abilities to create and manifest through our Spirit.

The 10th Chakra Is The Universal Chakra

As the name denotes the Universal aspect of our being resides in 10th Chakra. This vortex of our energy is proximately two and a half feet above the head.

Through this energy center, we are connected and part of the infinite flow of all creation, through us. When open and activated, the Universal Chakra will allow the feeling of our close alignment with the Universe and all that is.
Thus, we can develop a connection with the light beings in the universe. Additionally, we can merge in unison and alignment with our light body within this form, here on earth.

When this chakra is fully activated, it allows the 'Merkaba' light_body to be constructed, enabling us with the unlimited entrance to travel within the higher realms of spirit.

Through the Universal Chakra, we experience Divine healing balance in our lives and full access to the divinity of our souls'.

The 11th Is The Galactic Chakra

Our Galactic energy vortex is located proximately four feet above the head. When this energy center is fully open and activated, it allows the development of advanced Spiritual abilities.
Part of which is traveling beyond the limits of time and space, teleportation, instant manifestation, and more.

For now, here we can reach out anywhere in the realms of Creation and to communicate with higher dimensional light beings and Ascended Masters.
Therefore, we can bring higher healing, insights, and growth from the Galactic realm into our present existence.

When activated, through our Galactic Chakra, we can bring balance to the wide number of people. Everyone around us, including Mother Earth and the highest realms of spirit can benefit through our frequency and vibration.

The 12th — the Divine Gateway Chakra

This chakra center is the Divine light portal allowing our complete connection to the Source, therefore it is an open doorway to explore other worlds and realms.

Here we experience full ascension, complete oneness with divinity of our being, and divinity of everyone, and everything. Our full connection to the cosmos and other worlds is possible when this energy center is fully activated.

Through this vortex of energy we are the vehicle of love, peace, harmony, and ascension, enabling these greatest qualities to enter others through us.

All the levels of Divine and all the qualities of divinity represented by higher vibration beings may align with us here.

Activating the Divine Gateway Chakra will allow the Divine--Source Blessings to flow down our body to the Earth Star chakra. Thus, us as the vehicles, we are connecting the Light and power of the universe to the crystal core of the earth.

This unending loop of Divine awakening is working through our presence, bringing growth and our ascension with every breath we take.

In Conclusion

Utilizing wisdom and practicing awakening, opening, and activating the energy vortexes of our auric field with the body through the conscious breathe and visualization brings the awakening and transformation to our lives.

Considering that we are using our might in unison with Universal forces, it makes it most appropriate and in alignment with our original design. Our Soul Star Matrix and the plan are being initiated through this knowledge and practice.

11

Connecting The Six Chakras Within Our Body With The Six Chakras In The Auric Field

T his chapter explains how and why we can benefit by connecting and activating our 12 Chakras system.

We will explore why and how to connect the six chakras within our body with six chakras of our auric field and the wisdom behind this method for our advancement.

Among many benefits, knowledge with practice does the two things:

- It will increase our awareness, in the now moment

- At the same time, we can feel more connected to everyone and everything.

Additionally, the conscious circulation of the higher light frequencies from the universe with our auric field can greatly increase our physical body frequency.

In this way, we are aligning and assimilating the new frequencies of light into our physical forms, and the auric field.

The practice will ground, and connect us to Mother Earth. Our, I AM presence and our unique frequency and force, our message will awake.
We are actively enforcing our unique Universal light forces within.

Consequently, we are becoming important vehicles of light and love for our lives and the lives of others at this significant time.

What drives me most to do this practice is that we can bring in cosmic consciousness, and wisdom into our present lives. Ultimately, our hearts will open when we become the harbingers, and heralds of the higher levels of consciousness on the new earth.
Thus, we are taking an active role in evolving to our next best level and assisting others in moving forward into higher levels of consciousness.
Let us begin.

Earth Star Chakra And I AM Presence Within The Crystal Core Of The Earth

The best is to stand up; you can sit up, with your back straight, away from a surface, and the head is parallel to the universe. Keep your feet shoulders width apart, if standing or heals touching, if you are sitting in the chair.

Visualize the beam of light from the core of the earth, rushing up, throughout all 12 Chakras. The silver cord of light is continuing its way up and through our cosmic portals to all the universes.
The light is coming back down while clearing-up possible negative information from our auric fields back to earth.

Divine Gateway

Galactic Chakra

Universal Chakra
Spirit Chakra

Soul STAR

Crown Chakra
6th- Chakra

5th- Chakra
Heart Chakra

3rd- Chakra
2nd- Chakra
1st- Chakra

Eart STAR

By visualizing the beam of light for a few minutes soon, we can sense that the light force of the universe is successfully reconnecting and activating our internal Chakras. Also, our auric field is receiving the splash of cosmic light frequencies.

Continue by visualizing the silver cord of light is bringing up the frequency, and light from the crystal core of the earth, to your Earth Star Chakra.

In the 0-the Earth Star chakra, this light force is assimilating our unique frequency and connection with Mother Earth, while continuing up to the 1st Chakra.
Visualize your Earth Star chakra in brilliant white light, emanating and awakening your I AM presence invigorated by Mother Earth's unconditional love for a few seconds.

Joining The 1st-Root Chakra, With The 12th-Divine Gateway Chakra

When you are ready, move the focus to the 1st-Root Chakra.
Knowing that, the Root-Chakra is the foundational energy center for the whole body and the 12th-Divine Gateway Chakra is our Divine light portal, we want to initiate and activate this connection with the Source here.

Visualize these two energy centers light up and connected with a brilliant white ring of the Divine Source light. Stay with the visualization for a minute to ignite your connection with the Source, here.

When we are in divine-flow and presence, our earth's experiences are effortless and we are divinely guided. Therefore, here we are consciously affixing the universal force to the connection between our lives' foundation and creator's powers.
Through practice and consequently, the creator's

unconditional love and the light are becoming our light and flow throughout all 12 Chakras and the auric field, effortlessly.

We continue by visualizing the crystalline light from the core of the earth going up the central channel.

In the 1st–Root Chakra, the color is turning into a bright red vortex of energy rotating and emanating the light all away, to the 12th Chakra.

Here, in the Divine Gateway, the flame of light is bursting out and back down through the energy field.

The light is clearing up all that is preventing us from being our original divine self is washed away.

Circulate the crystalline light through the Root Chakra, up the central channel to the Divine Gateway Chakra, and back-down for a few more minutes.

Consciously Connecting The 2nd Chakra, With The Galactic Chakra

Once we have established the light and love of the divine energies within us, we are ready to move on to the 2nd Chakra.

The 2nd--Sacral Chakra is our second major foundational energy center. Also is located in the central channel of the body and between the 1st Chakra and the navel area.

The Sacral Chakra energy center is known to be in charge of our relationships with the outer world and our creative abilities. Thus, its energies determine our relationships, finances, and the overall alchemy of our presence on earth.

For this reason, it is wise to connect this energy center with the 11th Galactic Chakra at this time.

By connecting Galactic light-frequency with the 2nd Chakra we can experience more advanced abilities coming through our given traits and talents. Our creative force can be initiated and up-leveled with the Galactic light and frequencies from this and other galaxies.

To be exact, we are reaching out to the higher dimensions and realms of consciousness and bringing the wisdom and insights into our life here on earth.
Also, while practicing, we are bringing balance, harmony, and higher light-frequencies to others and Mother Earth, as well.

Visualize the Prana--the light force of the universe, coming upwards, from the core of the earth to the 2nd-Chakra. Here, the light is turning into a bright orange vortex, rotating and emitting the light, while continuing upwards and to 11th--Galactic Chakra.

The galactic silver light-energy and force are clearing up our auras and the central channels, coming back down.
At the same time, it's bringing in the galactic-light and frequency into our energy fields.

Stay with this visualization for a few minutes and until you can see, feel the central channel and your auric field recharged by the Galactic light and frequency.

Expand and experience your Galactic frequency field as you wish, for a few minutes.

Bridging The Solar Plexus, With The Universal Chakra

Now, we can move our attention to 3rd-Chakra.
The Solar plexus chakra is where the true power of our soul resides.
Therefore, let us invoke, and command this power by saying:
"Dear my Solar plexus Chakra, you are the seat and carrier of my soul's might. You have the power to connect to all

existence. Please, align my being with all creation and connect with it by joining with 10th–the Universal Chakra."

The Universal Chakra can connect and align us with all creation.

For this reason, we are initiating a bridge of light between our Solar Plexus and 10th-Chakra.

Ultimately, becoming one with all creation will help us to experience ourselves fully, here and now.

Besides, when we activate the light forces of the universes with our Sun in the Solar plexus, they can allow our Merkaba light body to be constructed.

Visualize the light coming up through the central channel to the Solar plexus. The yellow-golden light vortex starts spinning and rotating in the center of your body. The light starts to emanate its golden-rays all-the-way to the 10th–Universal Chakra.

Here, some feet above our heads, its joining forces with the light frequencies from all the universes.

Unified with our soul-light, the golden rays of light are coming back down, while bringing in the light-frequencies from all universes to our solar plexus and the auric field.

Connecting The Heart-Chakra, With The 9th–The Spirit Chakra

Let us bring attention to the middle of the chest, where Heart Chakra is.

The area between our physical heart and the Heart-Chakra is where our essence and the core of our being reside.

Therefore, our life can benefit greatly when we create a strong bond and connection between the Heart-Chakra and the 9th–Spirit Chakra.

Why is this beneficial to our journey?

Given that our heart center is our transformation, acceleration, and communication center holding all our talents, we want to connect and expand these gifts and abilities through our Spirit vortex and the auric field out to the world.

Secondly, remember that we have received the unique spirit for this life and the heart center connects us to our eternal soul. Therefore, the sooner we initiate the joining of our spirit and the soul as one and unified, we can experience the fullness of our being faster.

Besides, when these two energy centers are aligned and connected as a whole, we can communicate with the vast realm of spirit. This includes our direct joining with the Divine-Source within us, God-self us, in this physical form on earth.

When we can surrender and trust the flow of our spirit, it is a divine flow, and we can access and realize our soul's gifts and abilities to their full capacity here and now.

How to practice the Heart to Spirit connection?

Visualize the beam of crystalline light, going up from the earth through the central channel, and turning into a bright, emerald-green light, when it reaches the middle of the chest. The fluorescent green light is bringing harmony and balance to our hearts and all that we are.

Visualize all your gifts and abilities gathering and ready for exploration harmonizing here within the world of existence and the invisible power and the world of your spirit within the heart.

Here, and little above the Heart-Chakra, the vortex of light stars to spin and emanate, crystalline pinkish beams of light of our higher hearts activating.

Stay focused on your higher heart for a moment or two. Expand the feelings of the Higher Self presence and unconditional love for life and all beings rising within you. Surround in pink all that you are and you have to offer.

Before we continue with the light moving-up, and through the central channel, to the 9th–the Spirit Chakra, visualization of this expanded unconditional state and the love of our higher self heart continue.

Circularly, and in the 9th-Spirit Chakra, the crystalline-green-pinkish beams of light are turning back down and showering our auric fields with a brilliant light of our spirit and its higher heart presence within.

The light is ushering the new higher frequencies of love and light with the gifts and abilities of our spirit into the energy field.

Experience these light-frequencies for a few more minutes, and until you can feel and see all the crystalline particles of your spirit and its traits within the auric field liberated and free.

Consciously Connecting The 5th- Chakra, With The Soul Star Chakra

The 5th–Throat Chakra represents our ability to express our talents and gifts through a particular service to others.

For example, our gift to express through communication, speech, and can also be a talent not connected to vocalization and is still our expression in service to others.

For this reason, we want to create a bond between the energy center in our throat area and the Soul Star Chakra. Why is this significant for our lives?

Firstly, the 8th–Soul Star Chakra, carries the wisdom and knowledge of our soul's experiences throughout many lifetimes.

Secondly, when we have fully activated the Soul Star Chakra, the Creator's light flows through this energy center freely, allowing us to access higher realms of consciousness. Potentially, we can connect to the wisdom and knowledge from our previous existences.

Essentially, we are awakening and utilizing our soul's experiences into the current life, and share them with others through our service and 5th-Chakra.

How we can practice the 5th and the Soul Star Chakra connection?

Visualize the creators' light, the brightest diamond light flowing through your Soul Stat Chakra, and down the central channel, through the throat-chakra to the core of Mother Earth.

Feel or see, this brightest light-emitting and spinning a foot above your head and circulating back down and up, from the throat chakra energy vortex to the Soul Star chakra for a few minutes.

Circulate the crystal frequency-light, up and down, removing blockages from your ability to express the truth of yourself freely and fully.

All the while, the crystalline particles of light carry the knowledge and wisdom of your souls' experiences from other lifetimes too.

Feel free to expand the light-frequency field of your soul and the throat chakra to the left and the right, 11-22 feet around, see it emitting and expending the rays of light to many people through your service.

Meditate on ushering and developing your soul's abilities and experiences from this and other lives for a few minutes now.

Connecting The Crown-Chakra With The 6th-Chakra

The 6th-Chakra is the energy center connected to our Spiritual Channels and the 3rd Eye.
We intuitively, through images, telepathic communication, or direct knowing, receive insights for our lives and journey through these energy centers.
The non-physical nature of the 3rd-Eye and Spiritual Channels is represented by light frequencies.

Therefore, let us intentionally use the light to create the connection and activate our Spiritual Channels and the 3rd Eye abilities through working with the 6th, the Crown Chakra, and all the Chakras above the head.

Visualize the indigo-blue flame of light in the middle of the head in the pineal gland area. See the light twinkling, expanding, and contracting for a few minutes.
Now, move the indigo-blue crystalline light through the 6th and 7th Chakra in a circular motion, up and down, for a minute. See/feel the light balancing and harmonizing the left and right brain hemispheres when the increasing of the intuitive, telepathic, direct knowing and 3rd Eye abilities happen naturally.
Expand the light now, turning into a beam of violet light in the Crown Chakra and to the Divine Gateway. Visualize all the chakras above the head lit up and connected, operating in unison by the frequency and light of your spiritual channels and abilities.

In Divine Gateway the light is bursting out and coming back down, clearing all the chakras above the head and the crown with divine light. The crystalline translucent violet light is satiating the auric field. Stay with this visualization for a minute.

See and feel your Crown and the 6th Chakra in violet crystalline light expanding and forming crystalline high-frequency protection blanket and field for the whole body and the auric field. Stay with this image of you protected and invigorated by the light for a moment.

Summary

Although we have worked our way to the Crown, this is not the destination or conclusion. It is the rebirth and a beginning where the infinite unfolding of new experiences begins, all taking us to our ultimate goal, unification through self-realization and fulfillment.

Thus, advancing and developing the spiritual channels through practice can facilitate the realization and unification of our higher-self presence and purpose within this form. We have also brought the universal light and frequency to our 12-Chakras and the auric field, clearing out the negative entities, igniting our unique potential and abilities into our form and the auric field. At the same time, we have reclaimed our energy and frequency, creating a protective crystalline light energy field surrounding our physical form.

Consequently, our unique Soul Star Matrix is being ignited and united with our original design, here on earth, and it is now ready for expansion. When we experience the crystalline translucent nature of our auric field and work with 12-Chakras, our frequency accelerates beyond the physical.

As our body frequency is raised, the consciousness expands. In time, we find ourselves in the higher realms of consciousness and awareness, as fully awaken and aware multi-dimensional beings of light and love.

12

Ascension Of Love Consciousness To 'One Heart' 6D Consciousness

The Next Step in Humans Evolution Is 'One Heart' Consciousness

As part of the continued evolution of human consciousness, we are evolving through our hearts.

Specifically, humanity's awareness is shifting from being aware through our minds to being consciously aware through the heart.

The One Heart consciousness is the next step in our evolution and the awakening of 'one heart' in humans, on the New Earth, is our evolution to higher states of consciousness and awareness.

What is 'one heart' and why it is so significant at this time we are exploring in this chapter.

The concept of one heart follows from the wisdom that the

heart is the essence of our human being, thus living from the heart denotes the higher purity and quality of our lives in then our new reality.

To be exact, we are experiencing the expansion and liberation of our human consciousness through living from the heart.

I believe you can agree that this is a step forward to our next levels of awareness. It is a monumental shift on a global scale.

Maybe you have noticed that with the new higher frequencies of light on the Earth, the mass consciousness is transposing from an individual to a collective consciousness. People are becoming more aware and concerned not only for them but also for the well being of others.

Awakening Of The One Heart

As already discussed in previous chapters, we know that the heart determines what our experience of life is, and the level of consciousness we can meet the following is for our reflection.

On the scale of the ladder in our human evolution through the heart, there are three stages.

From the development and expansion of our personality heart in the middle of the chest, also known as the Heart Chakra. This energy center is an emerald green vortex and the wheel of our immediate concerns. The emerald green in color signals our necessary harmony and balance within and with the outer world.

The second stage is the development of the higher heart or the higher-self heart. This stage of our heart's evolution is when we go beyond our personality self and realize the Higher-Self heart or the Christ consciousness.

Also, referred to as our sacred heart, and it is rose pink in color. The rose pink color denotes the development of unconditional Christ love for all, oneself and others.

The third stage is opening and activating of the One Heart.

One Heart resides in the center of an upper chest and in-between the higher heart and 5th-Throat Chakra.

Once it is activated, its crystalline turquoise in color, emanating brilliant translucent crystalline light throughout the upper chest. It reaches out to all beings. Symbolizing our unified existence, merged in devotion and ever-present now moment it is emitting the frequencies of oneness.

One Heart is the heart without struggles, attachments, and separation, with no chains around. Liberated, just like the ocean, it is flowing freely.

Through its presence, it is setting free not only oneself journey but the journey of others, also.

The location and translucent turquoise color of One Heart symbolize two main characteristics:

Firstly, One Heart contains the heart of everyone and everything; thus, it connects to all things, the animate and inanimate beings. It is the feeling of eternal love, harmony, and bliss beyond time and space.

'One
Heart

6D Consciousness

One Heart

The One Heart Is The Heart Of Service To All Equally

Among all things, the One Heart is the heart of service to all.

Translucent turquoise tone represents the crystalline—fluid nature of one heart. Like water is, it symbolizes an unconditional service to everyone abundantly, without distinction.

As a drop of water that can go through the stone, the one heart characterizes significant potential power, forging vigorously, yet humbly, and equally in service to all.

The One Heart unites and brings things together.

With these qualities the awakening of 'one heart' allows us to access the sixth-dimensional consciousness and higher.

Additionally, it allows the creation of crystalline aura of the new human of light.

The 'One Heart' Meditation and Activation Practice is in Chapter 19, where you can find several exercises to support you in removing blockages, opening, and evolving your heart.

Access Your Highest Abilities, Through One Heart Consciousness

When our heart holds the One Heart frequency, we can retrieve all our talents and abilities. As the one heart has no chains around liberated, we can share our gifts freely with the world.

Furthermore, through One Heart opened and activated, our ability to bring the highest frequencies of love, care, compassion, and light to our lives and the lives of others is magnified.

In this way, we are the awakeners on the new earth, assisting many to evolve to the next levels of consciousness and awareness. Hence, helping them to access their soul's wisdom and abilities, to utilize them, in service for the highest good of all.

The New Earth–The Endless Potential

This is the main reason why the new Earth and the new Era have endless potential. They are meant to be the time of every soul light and highest potential.

Since we all have the heart and soul, it is doable vision for every soul to experience fulfillment after undergoing the new parameters. Also, we all carry wisdom and experiences from this and many lifetimes, our unique purpose to fulfill.

Given that we are living in the now moment, through the heart, in devotion, and the unconditional

state of the One Heart consciousness, our highest gifts are springing out, naturally.

Living in the now through the heart experiences stand for being in unity and harmony, with no separation within and with the outside world, is essential for the 'one heart' activation. Additionally, it means our freedom of not depending and expecting from the external world.

Instead, we are generating the frequencies of light out through being focused within and our potential powers.

Liberation For Humankind Comes From Within

Do you get the drift? The freedom and liberation for humankind is coming from the individual and it is within us.

Through feelings of unconditional love and undertaking, connected to all beings, Mother Earth, and the Universe we can experience our multi-dimensional conscious being.
The shift lies in the following:

Since the living from the knowledge and experiences solely derived from the mind is 3D consciousness.
The third dimension is precise, a human being in regards to space and time.

In other words, many people are still holding onto the old patterns, using mind power, agendas, and attachments to control others and outcomes.

The next step in humanity's evolution is 4D, which is a transitional period of purification of the mind, thought patterns, and emotions. Many people are currently going through this inevitable reconstruction within and with the outer world.

Considering that Mother Earth already carries the 5D frequency, they will be led to let go of the old ways and shift to their hearts' experiences in the now, where the higher frequencies of love and light are available to all and are leading to our advancement.

Our Hearts And Souls Lead The Way In The 5D, 6D & Higher Dimensions Of Consciousness

The easiest way to understand when we can move forward on our journey is through our hearts' evolution. Please, know when we're referring to our acceleration path, we point out to the spiritual heart–Heart Chakra.

To activate our 5th and higher dimensional being we go through a process of connecting fully to the crystal core of Mother Earth and the Cosmic frequencies through our Prana-tube, first.

After we feel grounded and connected through exchanging energies of love and light, with our beloved Mother Earth and the Universe above, we are ready for our heart's activation.

In other words, to experience our multi-dimensional self through the three heart's activations we have to be well-grounded in feelings of unconditional love and gratitude. Once grounded, we proceed with our first, second, and third heart activation. As explained earlier, we activate the personal heart first, then the Higher–Self heart, and the third is One Heart consciousness activation.

Furthermore, the pineal gland and our spiritual eye are activated, through this practice, to assist us in accessing the higher-self wisdom through intuition and 3rd eye visions.

The pineal gland gets activated when the left and right brain hemispheres are in proximate balance, which happens and it is ignited through the One Heart meditation.

In Conclusion

We can see once again, to experience and benefit from the shifts that are happening on earth the best is to allow the heart to lead the way. The awakening of One Heart will enable us to reach even higher awareness and higher levels of consciousness, the 5D, 6D, and higher.
When we live through the heart experience our life is our creation and depends less on the outer world.

Additionally, when we experience the world through the One Heart, we are filled with unconditional love and gratitude in service and union with all things.

We are mastering our physical form on the new earth. No doubt, through One Heart consciousness the new Golden Age is here, and we have arrived.

13

Is The Enlightenment Journey The Next Trend For Humans Evolution?

Humanity Is Awakening–Globally

Spiritual life and physical life are one. We are spiritual beings, and we choose our physical form to evolve to the next levels.
Humanity is awakening to this notion on a global scale.

Currently, we are relearning how to grow the light within our body, mind, and spirit.
Therefore, I can foresee the Enlightenment journey to be humanity's next trend in the decades to come.

Along with Mother Earth and all Universes, we are transitioning to our next levels, and the massive purification of our consciousness and sub-consciousness is prevalent.

The monumental shifts in frequency and light on earth are connecting us to our Super consciousness–Cosmic consciousness and being. This state is lifting off the remaining density of the old world and from our lives.

It is an uplifting time for all that are open and willing to change.

After all, the density from our bodies, minds, hearts, and spirit is transforming to more ethereal forms, and our auric fields are ignited by higher frequencies of the light on the new earth. We can experience a heightened awareness of the world around us and ourselves, and as a part of the Divine Source Plan for Humanity's ascension on earth.

The Plan for all is to become our natural original higher-self light and an embodiment of infinite and eternal higher-self love in form.
That is Ascension.

Purification On All Levels Of Life, Results In Heighten Awareness

This massive purification on all levels of our lives is causing us to experience life from our higher selves' consciousness and perspectives.

Our higher-self values are the new parameters on the new earth. The love, forgiveness, compassion, and care for the lives of others and our lives are in the air. Ultimately, Christ's Consciousness is awakening in many of us, on a massive scale

For this reason, the advancement to the level of our soul, mind, and body enlightenment is possible as we progress in time in our New Earth and this New Reality.

For those who still slumber, mainly, they have to get their personality selves out of the way and to open their heart to change. The new era is about transparency, willingness, and cooperation. It is the focus and development within, through the heart.

90

This shift is so significant, for just decades, and as well as the centuries ago, one had to eradicate the physical life and to commit completely to a Spiritual journey to evolve in this way.

Spiritual seekers were going to the remote mountains in Asia to reach the higher states of awareness and consciousness. They were isolating to purify and to experience what we can experience anytime, and anywhere on earth today.

In fact, or quite contrary, separation is inappropriate since, in unity within and with others, we ascend to our next level today.

Life On Ever-Giving Mother Earth And Our Roles

The easiest way to tap-into the acceleration process is to connect to Mother Earth and feel her unconditional service and love. Mother Earth is mother to all of us, her children. Therefore, grounding into her core qualities that are unconditional love and service to all, we can assimilate the condition.

Besides, as mentioned, Mother Earth already carries 5th-dimensional frequency and vibration, she chose the ascension. Consciously merge with her frequency to experience a higher frequency light within you.

Many times I hear people say, *I hope when I die, I go to Heaven*. At these times, I am thinking, and Heaven is right here on earth, now.

We have this abundant opportunity on the earth's bountiful blue and green expanded stage. So rich in what it has to offer to our performance and our unique roles.

So the idea is to tap into her abundance, beauty, and love and to emerge and build upon it in sincere love and appreciation.

Once we consciously choose the path of awakening and awareness through recognizing and freeing ourselves from the ignorance, resistance, and the attachments to outcomes, we become one with our higher-selves virtues. Our higher selves virtues are unconditional love, for others and ourselves, care, compassion, forgiveness, gratitude, harmony, and joy in service to all and our lives. All these attributes are already within us and ready to evolve to the next level when we are ready.

We Are Liberated And Limitless Without The Attachments

In this physical form, and this very lifetime, we have the opportunity to align and merge with our original eternal message—the Soul, and its infinite love and light.

The Divine, the Source seed within us is our always present light within. Staying connected, aligned, and guided from this eternal light-force within we are expanded and limitless in all aspects.

When we think of any attachments to outcomes and preconceptions on a situation or our ability are limiting this endless potential within us.

We are liberated and limitless without attachments and expectations. With love, devotion, trust, and through intentional personal growth and development, through contribution according to our original design, we can live the enlightenment journey on purpose, right here and now.

In conclusion, the source within us is limitless and abundant, only our attachments to something are limiting this potential within that is always ready to sore the heights.

The Steps Of The Enlightenment

We are limitless beings. How to embrace this truth and initiate our soul, heart, mind, and body enlightenment in this one lifetime?
Practically, there are a few steps to enlightenment.

To enlighten the soul, we firstly enlighten our hearts.

The pure heart in actions is where rubber meats rode. To get to a state of being and to emanate a pure love, compassion, grace, and light from our hearts at all times is being on the enlightenment path.

The next step to achieve enlightenment is to enlighten the mind.

We are to heal and transform our negative mindsets, attitudes, behaviors, ego, and attachments into higher frequency qualities. Thus, we develop purity, stillness, and peace of our minds through self-reflection, practice, and heart's awareness and consciousness moment-to-moment.

After we purify the hearts and minds, the soul gets uplifted, instantly.

With additional unconditional service to contribute to humankind and our collective and individual evolution, in time, we can enlighten our soul further. Thus, enlightenment is a process and evolution of the soul in a physical form.

Therefore, on the enlightenment path, also, the destination is not a motive, but the journey is fulfillment for the heart and soul.

The final step on the path of enlightenment is body enlightenment. As you can imagine, this step is the most difficult to obtain. To transform our physical body into the light-body takes total dedication, purification, and intentional practice.

Hearts Open, The Reality Is A Step To Knowing Ourselves And Others As Light

So, it is when our hearts open fully towards life, others, and ourselves that we start to accelerate and evolve.

Also, we become flexible, adaptable, open to receive all that life has to offer to us. One of the great benefits of living life through the heart experience is that we can see the truth on how to purify our soul, heart, and mind. In other words, we can observe others and ourselves, perceiving the truth to transform accordingly.

Additionally, the higher vibration states of consciousness, available to us when we live through the heart, allow our psyche to align and integrate the light of our eternal soul.

Our eternal soul, merged with the original design through the heart, carries the most appropriate light-frequencies available to us moment-to-moment. Therefore, we can experience the frequencies from the outer world, the New Earth, and the Universe through our hearts to be on the acceleration path in the timeless universe at all times.

When we are in this union with the eternal light of our soul, in the perfection of love through our eternal heart, we

are present in all dimensions of consciousness and awareness.
I suggest that you reflect on this knowledge and concepts.
It is a great practice and an experience.
To experience through practicing is to know.

The Enlightenment is as the word says, is the state of being aware and knowing oneself as Light.
In essence, we are light. The Source is light. Everything consists of different frequencies of light. Just being aware and perceiving the world in this way is a great place to start on the enlightenment path.

Thus, the idea is, and always was, to consciously assist the process of purification and growing the light within, through the heart, and our higher selves presence and virtues.

Being And Living Our Truth Through Love And Gratitude Is Service To All

The next significant point on the enlightenment journey is offering love, care, compassion, and forgiveness through our actions, deeds, and presence.
In other words, we can accumulate a good virtue through service and our contribution to the lives of others to fortify our path to enlightenment.

Consequently, when we remove all attachments to how things should be, we purify, and we do all we can in every moment, our life becomes enlighten and unconditional path of service in love and gratitude, by default.
Therefore, in this unconditional state we are serving others just by being our true selves presence.
Being and living our true original light and presence is akin to being of service to all.

Did you know, when we make others happy, healthy, or assist their path and contribute to the lives of others, we receive good virtue for our journey.

The good service benefits our physical and spiritual life. In physical life, good service can bring financial blessings, and on the spiritual path increases our soul standing and power.

In essence, our soul standing is increased when we live the life of merits, here and eternally in all existence.

Thus, on the enlightenment path, it is a necessary component to be of benefit to others and our collective.

In this way, we are opening the doors for the Divine and the Source unconditional service to flow through us and we are part of the extended light energy field that serves all beings.

Flexibility And Heart's Focus In The Quantum Field Reality

Purification of our hearts and minds consists of realizing the patterns of feelings and emotions, the ways linked to our need to control life and others, the ego, and attachment to things and outcomes.

All these lower vibration frequency states are up for transformation, to the frequencies of love and light, on the enlightenment path.

In general, everything that belongs to the old, linear, fixed, and controlled reality is not aligned with the enlightenment journey or the frequencies of the New Earth.

It is a choice we make on the acceleration path to transform darkness to light within our physical,

96

mental, emotional, and spiritual bodies, through focused awareness and intentional, deliberate practice to evolve.

Thus, the enlightenment path is a constant awareness and focuses on the acceleration path through a burning desire to merge in union with our original eternal light as a soul and its purpose, throughout all existences and dimensions.

I will explain the practice for the transformation of dense matter to light in the following paragraphs. The practical technique and how to practice it is in Chapter 25.

Similarly, Chapter 9 on conscious breathing, and Chapter 10 and 11 on 12-Chakras Activation and Connection, can be utilized for enlightening our soul, heart, mind, and body through practice.

Transmuting Darkness To Light Practice

The following is the ancient Taoist practice, I learned while studying with the Institute of Soul Healing and Enlightenment.

In its essence, the practice is a transformation of dense matter within our body, mind, and spirit to light. Consequently, it is the alteration cycle of the matter within our form to lighter and lighter matter, and to light-frequency. The light can be our original soul's light within, or the Source.

As I mentioned earlier this light within us is present yet, not always realized and utilized due to possible blockages, we carry. Among other benefits, this practice can help us in transforming density that is blocking our unification with the light within.

We can expand the wisdom of this practice, the transformation of matter to the Source light, to dissipate any dense matter within our lives to its more ethereal form.

Potentially, all attachments, negative ideas, and beliefs, as well as physical issues can be transformed to the light in this way.

All of the issues listed above consist of blocked matter, within our form, which ultimately causes the challenge and blockages in our lives.

I am still fascinated with this practice, its wisdom, the depth, and the effect that produces in my physical, mental, emotional, and spiritual life.

The actual Practice that can potentially transform the Matter in our body, mind, and soul into Light frequency is the five-step process:

– First—matter is produced in the Kidneys.

– Second—the matter alters to energy, in the spinel cord.

- Third—the energy transmutes to a message, in the head.

- Fourth—the message transforms into emptiness, in the heart.

- Fifth—the emptiness shifts to light, in the middle of

the chest, the Heart Chakra, also known as the Soul Temple in this Tao teachings.

Inevitably, and while practicing through focused intention, our consciousness also evolves to more pure, refined, and higher frequency consciousness.

What is obvious, the practice can assist the transformation of our physical body to the lighter body. This process is what the Enlightenment of our body, mind, and soul in its essence is about. Our goal on the path of Enlightenment is to become the light and more ethereal form in all aspects of being.

Reciting The Sacred Ancient And New Texts

There are more ways to assist our purification, acceleration, and ascension to the higher frequencies of light and consciousness.

Reciting, singing, and chanting sacred ancient and new texts or mantras is also the way to go into stillness or emptiness where we can experience the unity consciousness. Also, through stillness, we access our heart's and soul's intelligence, which is priceless for the enlightenment of our integrity and sovereignty.

The team is entering a condition of love and harmony with all creation and creating the space for great realizations to occur.

Besides, being a tool for going into a condition of

emptiness, these texts carry the wisdom and by repeating those sacred words we become them.

I found chanting or singing sacred mantras an effective tool for the purification process and entering the higher states of consciousness through stillness.
I suggest to everyone to find the mantras of your choice, a few you can relate to, and repeat them for 5-15 minutes, as time allows. You can create a mantra you would like to contemplate and repeat in your heart. We are all different but some things they work for most people similarly.

In other words, to accelerate we find different ways to enter the conditions of emptiness, unconditional love, and harmony with all things. Thus, in time we can enter higher awareness and unity consciousness, until they are our predominant state of being.

Final Thoughts On The Enlightenment

If we chose to do nothing, the alterations will happen at their speed in this new age of higher frequencies of light on earth.
Although, it is uplifting to realize that we can be co-creators of these expanded new higher frequencies of light on our planet through our presence and as an active contributor to the collective and our lives.

Now it is the time that we take action in any way we can for this purpose of creating love, light, and higher frequencies of consciousness for Mother Earth, Humanity, and all beings.

14

What Are The Benefits Of Sun And Moon For Humanity's Evolution?

Natural Phenomenon That Is Influencing Our Lives And Psych

The cycle of nature, the Sun and Moon, the Day and Night, the New and Full moon, is the most profound benefit to Humanity. They provide balance, alignment, and purify our lives, naturally.

The radiant golden rays of Sun, which hug and comfort the Earth, they ignite the fire and the light within each of our hearts with every new day.

Yet, at night, the cooling, gentle, silver light of the Moon, with its magical, sacred, feminine powers, graces and settles our beings with peace and inspiration.

This nature's perfect manifestation and perfection of balancing all that is feminine and masculine within us is the cycle of Day and Night.

With not much effort and just by aligning with it, and

recognizing its might, we can let this cycle of day and night, the Sun and Moon, alone, balance, heal, and re-set our soul, hearts, minds, and bodies every day, naturally.

There is another cycle of the Sun and Moon that when examined and recognized as an asset to our evolution, can bring even a greater union, and uplift within us and with the outside world.
That is the phenomenon of New and the Full Moon, every 28-30 days of our lives.
If you have not yet started benefiting from the magic of New and the Full Moon, I suggest that you start from today.

The Sun, the Moon, and the Earth are very old Souls; all three, they carry specific wisdom, knowledge, and different power within them, and on our lives. They are each, approximately 3.5 billion years old. So, to start benefiting from these celestial beings and their influence, it is never too late.

To truly dive into different possibilities, it is good to recognize some facts first.

The Sun And Moon Conjunction Their Impact On Human Psyche And How To Benefit From It

Generally speaking, the Sun influences and rules our consciousness, our actions, reason, logic, analytics of our being, the speech, too. These behaviors connect us to our Fire element and the masculine power, our Yang.
On the other hand, the Moon influences in our lives are associated and stimulate our subconsciousness. Such as our emotions, feelings, receptiveness, intuition, mood, and creativity. Thus, represents our feminine within that is associated with the Water element and our Yin side.

Every New moon is the new beginning when we have the opportunity to set the intention for our goals and areas of life that we wish to transform or realize and bring to life.

The Sun is the Star, very close to Earth and other planets of our solar system. If there were not for Sun, Earth would be a cold place.

Earth orbits around the Sun, and the Moon orbits around the Earth.

The different phases of the Moon, as they appear on the Earth sky, are caused by the different amounts of sunlight reflecting from the Moon's surface, while orbiting around the Earth, for 28-30 days at the time.

The New Moon happens when the Moon while orbiting, comes in between, and in alignment with the Sun and Earth. Thus, covers—takes over all the sunlight, leaving the side that is facing Earth in shadow. This phase appears as no moon, for about two days, and until the moon starts waxing, and New Moon appears.

The absence of the moonlight and the Sun's high influence causes our minds, hearts, and spirit to be supercharged by the power of the Sun.
This is a good time for us to set forth and invoke some new beginnings/realizations that we wish to manifest/realize in the following two weeks, of the waxing Moon time, until the Full Moon.

We are likely to be able to see clearly what it is that we wish to transform, or bring about in our lives.

This clarification and setting of our intent, while the New Moon, comes sort of naturally since our consciousness is exposed and stimulated by the Sun's impact on the earth also, the absence of subtle moon' power and light.

In the following two weeks, and the Waxing Moon period, we experience the increasing influence of the Moon' power on our subtle bodies and our subconsciousness.

At this time, our receptive, indirect, subconscious minds are more stimulated and tend to come up with the most obscure and mysterious ways to bring our desires that we set forth to live.

Let me share one practical example of how this may manifest in real life.

If you are a writer and you are writing a book and know you are missing some piece of information for your story.

You sort of know it is dormant, and it is stored somewhere in your memory bank. Your subconscious mind has it, and you can bring it forth and add the information to your story.

You may set your intention up, at the time of the New Moon, for this special information to be revealed to you.

During the waxing moon period, and the rising influence of the Moon, and giving that you are actively working on your story, it is likely that the information you requested surface and migrate from your subconscious to the conscious mind. Hence, you can successfully continue writing your book.

Using Nature Ways For Manifestation

At the same time, if we don't set a good intention for our progress, our subconscious mind may reveal some negative messages, memories, or experiences that can surface at and around the Full Moon.

Due to our whole system, the emotional and mental body

especially is highly sensitive under the influence of a rising moonlight, it is good to map out something good.

In essence, when we intend to enhance our gifts, and abilities, our activities and tasks at the time of the New Moon, so that we can benefit others and our lives, there is a great possibility that the constructive ideas will surface during the period of intense influence of the Moon on our subconscious.

Scientifically proven, and it is worthy mentioning, only 10% of our brain is consciousness, and 90% is subconsciousness.
This means that within our subconscious mind we carry a wealth of knowledge, information, and abilities, which are dormant, and we can potentially awaken them during these periods of intense Moon's influence on our psyche.

For the two weeks following the full moon, and the waning moon time when the moon is decreasing in her influence, we feel inspired to organize our lives. Spending time in revising, and modifying what we already have feels good and natural.
This is also a great time to break bad habits and reverse what is not in alignment with our purpose and plan.
I found the waning moon period powerful for spending more time reflecting and aligning with what is already present and with the source within.

In Conclusion On Power Of Moon Phases

Moon phases can assist us to purify, re-set, and re-calibrate our conscious, subconscious, and develop our super-conscious brain hemispheres. Thus, aligning them more with the potential powers of our soul, heart, mind, and body.

The moon cycles can help us expand our horizons. Consequently, we can see and feel more clearly how we are part of the whole and our connection to Cosmos and the Universe.

By connecting to nature, we can experience our divinity, the source within us, others, and our true nature and potential.
The connectedness with natural cycles and celestial beings is very nurturing, and it is a superfood for our soul, mind, spirit, intellect, and whole being.

The Solar & Lunar Eclipse Is When The Power Of Sun And Moon On Our Psyche Is Magnified

We have explored the impact of the New and the Full moon on our subtle bodies in this chapter extensively.

It is imaginable that while the Solar and Lunar Eclipses these natural occurrences have profound effects on Humanity's evolution, far-reaching and globally.

The unique impact on our human psyche and the opportunity for the clearance and balancing of our conscious and subconscious brain hemispheres are more profound during the Sun and Moon eclipse periods.

When the sun obscures the moon while the Lunar Eclipse, or vice versa while the Solar Eclipse the emanations are of greater light frequencies, so is the impact on our subtle bodies intensified, accordingly.

Thus, there is an opportunity for releasing the painful memories, sorrow, grief, sadness, traumas, and similar experiences that remained unsolved in our conscious and subconscious minds. During these natural occurrences.
As explained in this Chapter, we can resolve and settle

some of unresolved issues accumulated in our subconscious minds by tuning in, setting an intention, and being aware of these opportunities at the time of the Lunar Eclipse for instance. If we want to boost our consciousness instead, we can use the Solar Eclipse to utilize the feminine moon powers and influence to expand our consciousness in a particular way.

The lifting of the darkness from our psyche, at the occasions of Solar and Lunar Eclipses, is taking place globally, allowing more light from the Universes and Cosmos to spread and elevate our human existence here on Earth, widely.

So, it is good to prepare and benefit from these natural occurrences due to their potential powers that can facilitate the changes we seek at the moment. So is the case for many beings on Earth, sometimes causing the paradigm shift as well.

As a result, our human consciousness is being altered and we can find ourselves either more aligned with everything or possibly more disturbed if we get caught unaware and unprepared.
The yearly Eclipse Seasons are nature's free advancement for our evolution to higher states of consciousness and awareness that we can take advantage of, and we can benefit from.

15

Dawn & Dusk Empowerment Manifestation Zone, Time, Space, Sun, Human

When we enter the manifestation zone, beyond time and space, such as dawn and dusk, we experience the empowerment–the endless possibilities in our lives.

As time seems to stop, at these hours, the innate life and inspiration, they take off. The never-ending story of beginnings and the ends, on the horizons, of the setting and rising sun, are mighty.

What is that, which keeps us captive, at dawn and dusk?

The palpable feelings, so intense, yet, tangible enough that allow great realizations and discoveries to rise in our awareness at the hours of dawn and dusk.

Since I was young, I have this accord within, and with the rising and the setting sun, at dawn and dusk. It made me want to understand the deeper meaning of life and to contribute to the human psyche.

I have realized early on, at these times, I appear to be 'locked', and in the zone, beyond space and time. It is that place inside, where only magic reigns.

Why At Dawn & Dusk We Seem Locked In Time

No wonder, why?

We surrender and become one with the eternal moment, such as setting or the rising sun, when our spirit, through the heart, takes over the moment in time.

It is at dusk and dawn that we let go of the grip of our minds, and then, we enter the zone beyond the space and time through our hearts.
Hence, we can experience oneness with all life and opening of the heart.
This is an amazing realization that made my life a true miracle, in time.

Humans and all beings are blessed to have dawn and dusk on our side for the reflection and introspection times.

Each day we can enter the territory, beyond space and time, where we rejuvenate and recalibrate for our lives. These times allow us to experience the vastness of God-self us, being one with all creation, at the eternal, now moment such as dawn and dusk.
It is a perfect time to go deeper into the kingdom within a timeless, boundless space in our hearts.

Ultimately, when we are one with all that is, and in the now, through our hearts, we enter an eternal timeline, where all things are possible.
In other words, united within and with all life our realization and manifestation powers are magnified.

Nature has this infinite quality that can shift and expand our notion and consciousness regarding time, space, and us. Time, space, and form exist only in our thoughts. Therefore, time, space, and presence are the concepts of three-dimensional consciousness and reality. Where often we feel confined.

The sunset and sunrise, in their essence, are more like a fifth dimension or higher also, due to us being more inclined to harmony in the now, at these hours.
The mind being stunned by the beauty of the scene and the light of the setting sun, shuts down the thoughts, allowing our heart to open more.
It appears, once the heart takes over and connects us with the eternal presence of the setting sun, at those moments, we become one with eternity in the now.

Therefore, the vastness, unity and oneness realization can expand and open our hearts, and minds to experience of higher realms of consciousness and awareness.
Could be and can be any time, at this time on earth, but it happens that we are more willing to surrender to our inner world in peace, at dawn, or dusk.
So make it a great time to practice and experience being one with our limitless self, through the now and eternal heart when our manifestation powers magnify at dusk.

It is, when the heart thinks and expands, the things they manifest. Our most innate desires come to pass.

Therefore, keep this in your heart, at the times of dawn and dusk.
The sun's light is by far the most powerful influencer in our lives.
We want to utilize the sun's gifts and abilities with ours.

We can join with the Sun as one also because we all have the sun within us, the one in the Solar Plexus area. So, when we want to increase our manifestation powers, all we need to do is ask our sun, in the Solar plexus, to bless our vision. We can see, feel, or experience our sun, starting to rotate and expand.

It is joining together, as one, with the outer sun, and begins to emanate the golden rays of light. As a result, our vision and our psyche become one, a golden sun.

Then the magnetic nature of our inner sun will attract all things that are in alignment with our highest selves, to revolve around us.

At times of dawn and dusk, it is the perfect time for this visualization.

And so it is because we experience the vastness, oneness, and unity consciousness with all creation more easily at those times.

Additionally, the dimensions and levels of consciousness we experience are the result of our awareness in the now. Therefore, at eternal moments such as dawn and dusk, we connect to our eternal heart presence when we can through the moment potentially experience that we are present in all dimensions.

So, when our awareness is based and is about time, space, and form, we are in three-dimensional consciousness.

All our awareness beyond time, space, the body reference and when we allow ourselves to experience the eternal now, through the heart, we are being exposed to the magic, which is and always was the 5th dimension, and higher levels of consciousness.

Did you notice, our manifestation powers are related to our ability to completely merge as one with the given moment through the heart?

In truth, think about all our great creations are made, beyond time, space, and when we forget about our form in the eternal now through the heart.

It is exciting to realize that today, on earth, we are living steadily in the eternal timeline, almost at all times, and according to our will.
Sometimes I wonder, how many of us experience the same?
Of course, we still have the same joy and bliss while the sunset or sunrise at dusk or dawn.

Isn't it grand to be living on Mother Earth at this monumental time?
Still, at the dawn of the new era of Light, and one heart unity consciousness for all at hand.
In other words, it is time to relax at last.

To illustrate, a trick, with the sun that's coming down, I will share the poem I wrote, on the setting sun.

When The Sun Is Coming Down

When the sun is coming down
I am always there,
sitting, watching, imagining
this night and a new day.

This path of light is making me
very romantic and bright
It is quite a time
to imagine one I'd like to love,
today, tomorrow, at any time,
in the perfect glow of this burning light,
for what's this life without a loving one.

Since, the time I was very young,
I have this trick, with the sun that's coming down.
My constant longing for growth
is replaced by a longing for love
The real one that would never ask but satiate my soul.
In the perfect glow of this burning light
For what's life without loving one.

On that path of light towards me
I see the man of my dream
He is coming to stay
I see him talking to the Light
Imagining one he can speak to
only with his eyes
In that Land of Signs.

It's like romancing the stone I know,
but, I come to meet you there
In that land of love
On that path of glow
Very close to the edge
Where is the beginning
And where is the end?

Imagine what else you can find
When the sun is coming down.

16

Abundance And Flourishing, What We Are Vibrating To

We flourish in all aspects when we vibrate and emanate the frequency of our hearts and souls' unique message and purpose. Knowing that our emotional and mental bodies have the power to manifest the outcomes and experiences we live; it is the harmony and union with the passion of our innate being that we need to embody to produce abundance and flourishing in our lives.

Consequently, once our physical body starts emitting the frequency of our hears' and souls' desires and what we are focusing on, at the moment, the outcomes are our expanded being living in harmony and joy. The abundance is mirroring and unfolding in front of our eyes.

For this reason, it is essential to be aware and conscious of our feelings, the emotional, mental bodies, and our vibrational field energy.

So, to be focused within the heart chakra, where is our inner sanctuary of peace and harmony is what we attract to our lives. By gathering our feelings and emotions in a higher purpose, here in the heart center, we are the magnet to things and situations that are the most aligned with our highest destiny and evolution,

In the sacredness of our inner being, through the heart in consciousness and awareness of our original self's message, and presence coalesces to our highest destiny.

In other words, when our hearts and souls' intention is in alignment with our higher-self purpose, the heart naturally opens. The opening of the heart is a good signal of whether we are in accord or going against our highest plan.

Thus, when the heart is open, we vibrate the frequency of our innate desires, and we can expand in all aspects of life. So, our hearts determine whether we experience abundance or live in scarcity.

Harmony And Unity With Our Passion Produces The Abundance

Often the way we experience and project ourselves moment-to-moment is habitual. The good news is that it can be modified and reverted through living in reflection, also being aware and conscious of what we are sending out to the world.

In essence, we can observe our state and catch the feelings of separation and disharmony in moment-to-moment with our ultimate desires. Additionally, instead of indulging in the old program, our separation, and disconnection with the source within, we can consciously bring the focus back to the heart where our intent resides. The emotions of love and gratitude for our life's journey itself and the pursuit we undertook can bring us back to a condition of faith and fortitude.

It is the shift in focus from a struggle of the mental body to love and compassion of the heart and soul that works miracles at any time.

Sometimes, when this option seems unattainable at the moment, being aware and finding the light in all circumstances is the optional key.

I realized early on that human has to versatile in finding good, or the light, in all circumstances. Moreover, we have to recognize the causes on our own instead of looking out-there for all the answers. Simply because out there is the reflection of our world within. As well as, the experiences we live are individual, and we are led to all situation on purpose. Therefore, taking responsibility and going deeper looking for the answers and causes of what we are experiencing is paramount for our growth.

Thus, through the heart, and evoking the feelings of love and compassion for what we already have, we can consciously transform our experiences by emitting love and gratitude to our world. **There is no significant progress for us humans without self-love and taking responsibility through action**.

The Power Of The Light Within Is Flourishing

To be a conduit of the frequencies of love and light from the source within us is a universal service. Given that being in this state of harmony, we benefit others, too. Therefore, as soon as we are in alignment with our higher selves aspects and sending forth the frequencies of love and harmony, the universe is responding by gifting us with virtue to manifest our desires, and more abilities to offer more service.

When I learned the Law of Universal Service, I understood it so well and resonated with, because it is the truth you can experience it to know.

116

This truth and wisdom alone can save so much trouble and turbulence within today's society if more people know and practice it.

The Law of Universal Service is as follows:

Serve (create a good cause) a little, receive a little blessing from the Universe, the Divine, and the Source.

Serve more, receive more blessings.

Serve unconditionally receive unlimited blessings for your journey.

Therefore, service in benefit to others is the fastest way to accumulate good virtue and change our frequency and vibration. Beneficent actions and good deeds transform our presence to a higher frequency field when we can inevitably attract abundance or transform the desired aspect of life.

The holographic field of the Universe gives us what we put out through our presence and actions. Our Auric fields carry all our feelings, intentions, actions, and performance. For this reason and until we completely purify and align our physical life with the light frequency of our soul's purpose and the quantum field of reality, we train by being aware and adjusting what we are emitting to the field with our presence and deeds.

Our treasure is our unique frequency of light within. So, by connecting, and living this source of light within, we become our original light. Like this, in unison, we attract the most appropriate circumstances for our highest good and the good of others. We attract the things that are best for our evolution. Notice that we attract not what we expect or assume that it belongs to us, but what naturally flows in, and that which is most appropriate for us to evolve further.

Knowing to accelerate or transform, we usually have to recalibrate, amend, and improve, when after our new frequency brings us a new the most appropriate resolution. So, we endure the moment, revising in love and gratitude.

Also, having patience is critical for progress.

There is a saying: *Patience is the mother of science.*

Thus, if we want to master any aspect of life, we develop patience and persistence.

We need a lot of patience to evolve in any area of life. The same applies to attracting abundance and flourishing for our journey.

Attracting Abundance By Altering Projection Through Heart Center

Therefore, the abundance we do not necessarily have to acquire.

It is something we can adapt by changing our frequency and what we are emitting.

How do we modify and alter our projections in the quantum field of reality?

We come back to our heart centers and feelings of harmony and excitement about our passion and pursuit at the moment. In other words, we focus on things we already have and are excited about..

We do things that easily connect us to the flow of our original light and purpose within.

This flow usually happens when the mind is not controlling.

When we let go of programming and what an outcome should or could be like, we enter the flow of our innate being.

For some people walking in nature or biking, for many, can

be dancing or writing in general any action can produce flow.

Everything that we do with passion and excitement, means a heart-felt experience, can connect us to our original light and flow within.

Being In The FLOW Is Flourishing And Abundant

As I pointed out, there are many ways to enter the flow of our heart and soul. One of which is the_heart and soul movement.

It is the movement or dance when we let our hearts and souls lead the way. Our mind is quiet and not in charge.

By practicing this concept, doing any activity, we have the opportunity to experience how good can feel to be led by the heart and soul.

The truth is that when we are in the frequency of our heart and soul, we automatically live the abundance of all that we are.

Without having the mind in the way, all the knowledge and wisdom, from this and other lifetimes, come alive through us in this flow of our intent from within.

For this reason, we are the wisest and more abundant when we do not try hard to precisely figure everything out, instead, we allow the flow of our innate being to attract things in grace and ease.

The Layers Of Our Purification & The Wise Light Being Within

This is simple, although why we often struggle to project our lives into abundance and flourishing in all aspects?

One reason is that we have to grow into abundance and flourishing, like anything else, they are an on-going process and have layers.

Our hearts and souls carry the messages, and memories from all existences. Consequently, it takes time for all of them to purify, modify, and align in a union with our current existence and tendencies.

For example, what we can do, also, to assist the process is to align with and evoke the memories, times, and lifetimes when we were great contributors in a particular aspect we desire to fortify.

As we learned in the previous chapters, the heart is also the bridge to our soul, and the center of transformation, healing, communication, and the key to overcoming the challenges.
Therefore, when we experience a lack in finances or another aspect, we consciously bring the focus back to the heart, where our wise, light, and abundant, all-knowing being is present for guidance.
In this way, we can receive additional wisdom and knowledge to help us prosper and evolve.

Consequently, when we align with our higher aspect of being, through the messages within our hearts and soul, our life becomes more harmonious and abundant. Only thought and mind can make things appear contracted and limited from what they are capable of expanding into the endless potential.

One of the purposes of this manual is to expand our consciousness to the potential within us and the outside world. Where abundance and flourishing are our ability to vibrate, adjust, and align with the frequency of expansion and what is for the highest good for many that ultimately is the highest good for us, too.

17

Soul Movement And Dance

Soul Dance and Movement is revolutionary wisdom and practice of Soul Power teachings.

It is a movement exclusively guided by the heart and soul. For this very reason, it can assist in our healing, rejuvenation, acceleration, and longevity path.

Due to our knowledge that the soul can heal, itself and others, it is a powerful transformation method.

Distinctly, through soul dance, we can easily access higher states of consciousness and awareness. We can experience Heaven on Earth at this significant time, of our evolution and many changes of the outside and our inner world.

The practice proceeds from far-ancient times, after Chinese Traditional Medicine, used it for healing and rejuvenation, when finally, it is revived again in Soul Power teachings.

As pointed out, the Soul movement and dance are movements guided explicitly, by our soul. Consequently, it is an expression of our souls' frequency in action.

For this reason, it is very pure, untouched by logical thinking and mind; it is a connection with our higher-selves expression at the moment we dance.

Because our higher-self aspect is directly linked to the vastness of the Universe, the Divine Source within us, it makes the soul dance/movement a sacred practice and we can radiate the unconditional qualities of love, gratitude, and devotion throughout our whole being.

Also, through soul movement, we emit divine healing, expansion, and unification throughout our whole system.

Considering the above traits of soul movement and dance are also bringing higher frequencies of divine pure love and light to everyone around us, our community, and Mother Earth. That makes us active participants in accelerating the frequency on our planet and creating Heaven on Earth frequency and vibration for others also.

Therefore, the soul movement or dance by its nature is to have a significant place in humans evolution to the next levels of consciousness and awareness.
Many people will enter and understand the notion, course, and significance of the new era, and our new reality, more spontaneously through their movement guided by the heart and soul. The needed shift in the consciousness of masses can happen sort of effortlessly and in the flow.

Therefore, the release of unnecessary feelings and emotions blocking human evolution can be resolved through soul movement or dance. Thus, it is one of the top tools for awakening and manifesting more of our abilities in this far-ancient era return.
Here, we have our soul in action, taking lead through the heart and movement, ushering our presence, gifts, and talents in the New Earth and the new era of light.

While we soul dance, we can also feel that we are not alone. If our spiritual channels are open, we can see or feel other souls are dancing with us.

That is first because of the Divine, other light beings, stars, planets presence through our higher self-aspect. Secondly, as any ancient technique, performed in many different epochs, it carries the spirit and power of those times.

Bringing Heaven To Earth Through Soul Movement And Dance

The crux of this unique soul power technique is that the movements we make have no choreography or preplanned action but it is an organic expression of our soul, the soul of the dance, and the moment itself.

Therefore, connected like this and inflow and unison with our heart and soul, we can receive messages that are tailored for our acceleration journey at that moment we soul dance.

In other words, due to an expression deriving from our essence, through the heart, we feel connected within, with all creation, and we can receive unique messages and guidance from our soul and other advanced spiritual beings that can benefit our journey.

Consequently, soul dance/movement is a form of communication between the higher realms of spirit and us in action, through infinite love and devotion.

Communication happens spontaneously and in the flow of the movement or dance. Often, you can experience feelings of realization or knowingness about a particular aspect of life.

So, do not force or expect messages. They come effortlessly and as a result of your love and surrender in the moment of soul dance. You might hear the word or two, maybe see the image in your mind's eye. In any order, guidance and messages come as a reflection of your devotion to the task at that moment.

What Are The Key Points In Soul Movement And Dance?

The main point for soul movement and dance is to allow the body and hands to move freely and in the flow as an expression of our heart and soul. We avoid logical thinking and the mind's tendency to interrupt the flowing by directing the movement.

In the second place, do not judge your movements and dance. Stay focused within and on the point of the practice that is to release excess emotions, feelings, and any attachments from your body, mind, heart, and spirit that keeps you bonded and constrained in your day-to-day life.

Often being practical and brave in what we do is essential for our growth and necessary life changes.
Thirdly, we do a simple invocation to initiate our soul to action, like this:

Dear my beloved soul, I love you. Please, guide my movements/dance to remove blockages from my_____ state your request or just say my life and my journey.

After the invocation, just start moving with grace and ease, flow your feelings. Paint the picture and what you feel through your movement.
If you notice that mind's directing or editing how you should move, just bring the focus back to your heart. This conscious shift in focus will allow your heart to take the lead back to the soul's expression.

It is enough to keep in mind that editing the movement/dance will stop the flow and healing power. Therefore, it does not matter what movements you make, as long as they are an expression, in the flow, of heart and soul they will help you accelerate or heal.

Secondly, trust that your soul knows exactly how to move to promote healing and transformation for you. Relax and let the soul lead the way to your next level of consciousness and awareness because it knows how best to assist you.

The method is from far-ancient time, more than 1000 years old, serving many to their unification and transformation within so trust its power.

Additionally, stay in the feelings of love and gratitude for your journey and the **dance of your soul** is a great way to be in the flow of authentic self-presence.

You might notice that your awareness of the movements is increasing in time through practice, and it is what we want. Being more aware in the moment-to-moment is what we want, and is what leads to our acceleration and expansion of consciousness in all aspects and all moments.

Benefits Of Soul Dance And Soul Movement

It is amazing to know that something so enjoyable and uplifting, as soul movement and dance is, have many benefits for our life.

In my experience and since I started releasing my imbalanced feelings and emotions through Soul Dance, I have experienced a rebirth.

I have completely healed and at this time of my journey, I am in the escalation process on all levels.

So, as though the list can be long, I will point out some main benefits.

Firstly, healing takes place in the area of our life and character where we need to change the most. No wonder, our soul knows best where do we have the most blockages.

These blockages accumulated from our negative mindsets, beliefs, and attachments will go first. Negative memories, traumas, and unpleasant experiences will heal and dissolve to light through the opening of the heart while soul dancing.

Our soul dance will transform any darkness within us to the next appropriate frequency of our whole being, fast.

We will notice that our body feels lighter and more flexible due to the release of negative dense energy and matter from our system.

Unification In A Condition Of Love And Gratitude Through Soul Movement

I mentioned earlier, that soul movement impacts our whole body.

Our all systems, organs, the cells start vibrating and radiating the higher frequencies of light generated by our soul through its movement.

The more negative information we release from our body, through our heart and soul in action, the more vibrant, and more flexible we become. When one day, we know it, we are healed and restored to our original potential.

This is the truth, as soon as we let go of set concepts and we move in the condition and the flow of our love and gratitude within, healing escalates fast.

After we heal, our body's frequency starts to increase further, and the unification process within, and with the outer world, begins.

You can be surprised how fast your immediate issues will dissipate or vanish. In less than one year we can be amazed by the progress in all areas of our lives.

I know this transformation happens because we are allowing the heart and soul to express the self, without constant demands from our minds.
It is the new perception and dimension for life that we acquire through the practice of being in our flow while the soul move and dances.

At these times of turmoil in our society, many people are becoming more rigid in their bodies and minds. This stiffness comes mostly from the mind's desire to control outcomes and our attachments to something, rather than what already is.

These old programs and negative believes can be released through 5-10 minutes/per day of soul movement or dance easily.

Even though the soul dance may have more benefits than the soul movement, because of possible greater flow through dance. They both are very effective for removing the blockages and developing excitement and joy for our life and pursuit.

Boost Energy, Vitality, Stamina, And Immunity For Life's Demands

The next great benefit is that our energy, stamina, vitality, and immunity are increased through soul movement.

We know that our energy and matter, for this fact, are created by the cells' constant vibration. When the cells contract, they generate energy, and when they expand, the matter is produced.

We are in good health when this energy and matter transformation is in proximate balance. For example, if we experience weakness or tiredness our energy and matter transformation is impaired. Similarly, if we have inflammation, cyst, or tumor we have an excess of energy in that part of the body, again our cellular vibration is impaired.

The soul movement and dance can stabilize and normalize the cellular vibration and promote free energy flow throughout the body.

Thus, our immunity system, as well as the stamina, vitality, and energy level are boosted and promoted.

Once we heal our soul, hearts, minds, and bodies through this enjoyable act the acceleration begins.

The most significant benefit is our opportunity to accelerate to higher awareness and levels of consciousness. Due to the critical time we live in our continuous effort to support the evolution of the collective and our progress can be multiply through soul guided movement or dance.

Therefore, let us start releasing our negative emotions and attachments to live in the ever-present glorious now moment, through our hearts and soul in action.
Let us bring and share our love and light with Mother Earth and others, raising the frequency and vibration for all.

Part Two

More Practical Techniques For Our Evolution

18

Forgiveness Practice

F orgiving others and self help us advance to our next level faster.

Forgiveness practice carries a pearl of profound wisdom that I know can help us in removing the immediate disharmony causing issues in our life's experience. We transform blockages to evolve faster in our lives by practicing forgiveness.

It is quite natural; if we are stuck in one place for some time most likely, we carry blockages in our body system that we have to release to move to the next level. If these blockages do not transform to lighter frequency or heal, one way is through forgiveness practice; we can stay in the same spot for a while. Even if we move a bit, without releasing the root causeof our struggle, we can attract the same problems over again because we are vibrating the same frequency and message.

Through forgiveness practice, we sincerely reflect on the core of our issues that lie within us.

Let us explore further the significance of offering forgiveness and asking for forgiveness concerning our lives.

Advancing Blockages Through Forgiveness Practice

When we experience challenges in any aspect of life, this means that there are negative memories--the messages that are causing us to vibrate against our highest intentions. So, we attract what we vibrate-out to the world. Therefore, if we are vibrating the frequency of disharmony, in any aspect, this is the experience we live. It is simple and straightforward yet, to realize and transform an issue takes work, patience, self-love, and self-reflection.

If you would like to self-heal and transform blockages from your life, the forgiveness practice is the fastest self-healing method I know.
Why?

Firstly, when we are performing forgiveness for our issue we have the time to reflect on ourselves in regards to the disharmony we experience.
Where do the attachments that keep us bound, are coming from?
Know that they are negative memories from this or the previous lives. These messages are stored in our cellular vibration and can be released easily through sincere forgiveness. They are ready for transformation when we are ready. Thus, removing these negative memories, ego, attachment, and more can create space for our advancement.

So, the forgiveness practice can facilitate this transition from a blockage to the light frequencies of love, compassion, and forgiveness.

Secondly, when we forgive the souls that have hurt us, we release them from the bondage of karma law of cause and effect. As a result, this release significantly benefits

Dear Souls whom my ancestors and I
have harmed or hurt in any of our lifetimes
I Love you.
Please, forgive my ancestors and me for all
the harm we have caused you in this or our
previous lifetimes.
I am truly sorry. If I can turn back time
I would never make the same mistakes, again
Please, forgive us. Please, forgive me.
And if you ever harm my ancestors and me
I forgive you, unconditionally.
You do not own us anything
I set you Free completely and undonditionally
Please, receive our forgi andveness.
Let us join our hearts and souls together
To create a world of Love, Care,
Compassion,, Harmony, and Cooperation
And in Unity to birth the New Earth.
Thank you, Thank you, Thank You.

Forgiveness Invocation short, general

their soul journey and evolution. In other words, by offering forgiveness to others that hurt us, we are setting them free, when they can more smoothly continue to evolve. The release is taking place on the soul level, first, when the physical manifestation follows through their lives' experiences.

Thirdly, we ask for forgiveness from the souls we have harmed previously to please release us of bondage. This is when we create harmony within the challenge or an issue, on the soul level.

It is helpful to stay with this scenario, a few minutes, to offer sincere love, forgiveness, and to receive messages concerning the occasion we experience disharmony. As you can imagine, this exchange of feelings and emotions, through love and forgiveness, is the key point of the practice. Also, the invocation is essential; a short version of a general forgiveness practice is in the enclosed image of the previous page.

You can notice, in the general invocation, we include our ancestors and the ancestors of those involved in our encounter since their message and actions are within our cellular vibration.
In other words, sometimes we experience challenges because of our ancestor's negative deeds for the given problem. Thus, by including the ancestors of both parties, we multiply the effect of forgiveness practice.

So, as you can see the release and healing are taking place on many levels.
When we become one with a challenge and surrender to it, while offering heartfelt forgiveness to all people and things that are causing this issue, in this and other lifetimes, helps the release of negative emotions, feelings, and memories in our psyche and the heart concerning the experience. Also,

the same happens to those we are exchanging forgiveness with, on the soul level.

Naturally, the problem can arise between two people, a group, or regarding an aspect of life, health, finances, business, relationships, and what we suffer from, can be uplifted in the process of sincere forgiveness.

Also, instant, short forgiveness at the moment we see the conflict arising, we can silently do quick forgiveness for the issue at hand. Sometimes, the instant forgiveness contemplation can immediately change the feeling and the course of a situation.

Extended Forgiveness Invocation

The following example is the extended Forgiveness practice, we can do when time allows and we have extra minutes to dedicate to visualization and reflection. In other words, we have time to go deeply into a condition of love, forgiveness, and compassion in surrender.

In this version you will notice that in the first part we ask the Divine, the Source for forgiveness for the matter of our request, in the second part we are asking all souls that our ancestors and we have harmed, to forgive us. In the third part, we offer forgiveness to all those who have harmed us.

Three times thank you, after each request or offer, is: first thank you is to the Divine and the Source, the second thank you is for all other being of light and Masters, and the third thank you is to our soul.

Visualize all souls connected to an issue in golden light in front of you, and go into a condition of love, appreciation, and sincerity in peace.

Dear Divine, the Source, Dear countless planets, stars, galaxies, and universes, I love you, honor, and appreciate you.

Please, forgive my ancestors and me for the mistakes we have made against you, in our lifetimes together, causing blockages in my life today.

I am sincerely sorry, I ask for your forgiveness. Please, forgive us please forgive me.

I have changed, I have purified, I will contribute to assisting humanity through my good service to make others happier and healthier.

Thank you for your forgiveness.

I am grateful for all future opportunities to assist others with my gifts and talents you gifted me for this purpose.

Thank you, thank you, thank you.

Dear souls, whom my ancestors and I have harmed or hurt in any of our lifetimes.

I love, honor, and appreciate you.

Please forgive my ancestors and me for any harm or hurt we have caused you.

I am sincerely sorry, and I ask for forgiveness. Please, forgive us. Please release me from the bondage that I can move forward on my journey.

If you can forgive us, I promise to do good service to all and to assist others in their lives. I am grateful for your forgiveness.

And if you ever hurt or harmed my ancestors and me, we forgive you totally and unconditionally. You do not owe us anything. I set you free completely, please, receive our forgiveness.

Let us join hearts and souls together to create a world of Love, Peace, Care, and Cooperation to birth the New Earth.

Thank you, thank you, and thank you.

I remember when I first looked at the Forgiveness practice sheet, similar to this one, I received from Soul Power Institute while studying, it seemed quite complicated to me. Although the logistics are simple, you are asking for forgiveness from all those you or your ancestors have harmed or heart, and you are offering forgiveness to them.

It is good to start with asking the Divine and the Source to forgive us in regards to an issue. Invoking the Divine, the Source, and other light and celestial beings helps us going into a sincere infinite love and compassion more easily. You can choose the Ultimate Creator, Universe, and Cosmos, Star beings, whomever you believe in and has the higher power for you. The effect is the same.

The practice is about us, becoming one with a challenge and surrendering in sincere reflection, love, gratitude, and forgiveness to all people and things concerned and causing the conflict.

Also, we are asking for forgiveness from those souls that we have harmed or hurt, releasing them, and in this way we are creating harmony within an issue, on the soul level. Including our ancestors and the ancestors of others helps, since we release ancestral negative messages, which increases the effect of forgiveness practice. The theme is that we clear the space between us and an issue on the soul level when physical manifestation follows.

This is a profound truth, I learned and experience using this soul power technique. Once we remove negative information, especially from our soul, heart, mind, and body on the soul level for any issue, we settle in peace, when things in real life can transform.

Forgiveness For The Aspect Of Life—Health, Finances, the Love Life

When we are experiencing difficulty in the aspect of life such as our health, finances, business, or difficulty finding true love, or any other, we do a forgiveness practice for that aspect. Since the blockages are caused by negative memories when we were hurt, or hurt others in the same way. Forgiveness will soothe the wounds and clear and prepare the space for transformation.

Therefore, offering forgiveness to all those people that we have hurt, or our ancestors have hurt, and asking for forgiveness from them, will remove blockages from the aspect, on the soul level.

The more we sincerely reflect on this situation, in love and forgiveness, the more negative emotions will be released and greater chance for transformation is possible. The essence is to as deeply and sincerely as we can assess the situation and offer love and forgiveness as it is happening right now, in front of us through visualization and retrospection.

You will be amazed by the positive effect that offering forgiveness on the spiritual level has in real-life situations.

The crux of the forgiveness practice is to satiate the core of the issue with love and compassion. The spiritual level is effective due to creating a deep feeling, living, and believing it as it is happening while affirmation.

The forgiveness affects our whole system to unwind and surrender. Consequently, forgiveness is closely connected to our Heart Chakra and the Sixth Chakra–in the middle of the head. Through the heart, we experience heart to heart connection with an issue or a person we are creating forgiveness with.

Dear Souls whom my ancestors and I
have harmed or hurt in any of our lifetimes
In regards to my struggles with _____.
I Love you.
Please, forgive my ancestors and me for all
the harm we have caused you in your _____,
in this or previous lifetimes.
I am truly sorry. If I can turn back time
I would never make the same mistakes, again.
Please, forgive me. Please, forgive us.
And if you ever harm my ancestors and me
in this way, I forgive you, unconditionally.
You do not own us anything
I set you Free completely
Please, receive our forgiveness
Please, forgive us
Let us join our hearts and souls together
To create a world of Love, Care, Compassion,
Harmony, and Cooperation
And in Unity to birth the New Earth.
Thank you, Thank you, Thank You.

Forgiveness Invocation for an aspect of life

Through our brain and the Sixth chakra, we are making it as real as it is happening right then.

The more blockages we release from our emotional, mental, and spiritual systems, the more we become intuitive and liberated within and for the issue or challenge. Releasing resistance and disharmony from our lives through forgiveness practice will harmonize our left and right brain hemispheres, due to clearing negative memories.

When left and right brain hemispheres are in proximate harmony, the Pineal gland produces serotonin and other endorphins that create feelings of happiness and joy.

The Pineal gland, a cherry-sized energy center in the middle of the brain, is also crucial for developing our intuition and Third Eye's abilities. So, if we want to develop our spiritual channels, in particular the 3rd Eye Channel, forgiveness practice is the facilitator.

To understand the core qualities and the essence of this simple technique to transformation, we have to practice it as often as we can.

The benefits for our unification and transformation are enormous on all levels of our existence, once we learn to surrender in love and appreciation and experience the benefits of the soul-to-soul connection in exchanging forgiveness, on our physical life.

Since it works, I advise you to give forgiveness a chance, it is a powerful tool to self-remove blockages from our system and our lives. Also, as we learned it is the way to transform our immediate challenges in life. Anything you can think of you can alter and modify through offering forgiveness.

As with any practice when we go deep, and become one

with, forgiveness brings healing and inner peace. Therefore, the desired transformation follows.

Do not let it take you two years to implement it. It took me that long to understand the depth and to actualize it in my daily life.

I did experience profound benefits and instantly when I realized the essence of it and why forgiveness creates a complete oneness within and with the encounter.

Unlock The Door Of Manifestation Through Forgiving Yourself And Others

Open your heart and your mind to receive and reflect on this information and then follow your intuition and guidance to proceed.

Life always serves us with the occasions or challenges that will assist us the most to move forward on our path. In other words, the challenges are our tickets to realizing the necessary change and what we need to learn and understand.

Many times doing the Forgiveness practice can prevent some of the disturbance/occasions to occur in our lives. Due to this fact, we have changed our frequency through practicing forgiveness and have spent time reflecting on the issue.

In Summary, Why Forgiveness?

In the Power of Soul wisdom, forgiveness practice is the key technique to self-transform for the better.

In essence, whatever we are suffering is caused by our frequency and vibration or the message we carry within us. The way to change our vibration is to transmute these negative memories, messages, and information to higher frequencies of love and forgiveness.

Our eternal soul brought these messages to this physical form and this life so that they can heal and transform to light.

One of the shortcuts to this transformation is doing a sincere forgiveness practice. We offer forgiveness to all beings, and things, that our ancestors and we have harmed, in this or previous lifetimes, in regards to the experience or challenge, and we ask for forgiveness.

Forgiving And Being Forgiven The Benefits

Forgiveness practice is a practical way to self-clear our negative karma. What is Karma?

Karma is the record of services, we carry within us, and it is manifesting through our cellular vibration and our overall message.

Negative Karma is the debt—negative message we own to others. Particularly owned to those whom we, or our ancestors, have harmed or hurt in the areas of our sufferings.

When we forgive others, we release them from the debt from our ancestors and us. By setting someone free, we help them on their evolution. Simultaneously, we create a good virtue for our progress and growth.

In other words, we are setting others and our life free from the karmic law of cause and effect, creating good karma for all.

Good karma is a record of good service that our ancestors and we have accumulated over the lifetimes.

When we offer care, compassion, love, forgiveness, and when we help others progress we create good karma.

So, it is best to work on one challenge at a time and to go into a condition of sincerely offering our Love and Forgiveness. We reflect in love with those whom our ancestors, and we have caused suffering and struggle, previously.

Sincerity Moves Heaven When It Comes To Forgiveness

Be sincere and open your heart to give and receive forgiveness. There is a saying: *Sincerity moves Heaven.*

This is true since whenever we are truthful and honest to others and our lives, we benefit from the situation.

Additionally, each time we become one with what we do, we receive a lot of energy, and we feel uplifted.

Significantly, through sincere forgiveness practice, we lose the attachment to the outcome since we shift to a zone larger than life.   We already know, the attachment to outcome is preventing us from manifesting what we desire.

When Forgiveness?

In essence, forgiveness practice can assist us in letting go of the grip on our life.

Do the forgiveness practice for your challenge once a day, for 3-15 minutes.

Take notes, and share your experience and progress with others. To share is to serve others who also need a transformation and growth.

Apply forgiveness to the physical, mental, emotional, and spiritual aspects of life. Do forgiveness to transform your relationships and finances.

To experience is to believe.

I experienced forgiveness practice as the best practice to transform my whole life.

I wish you can experience and benefit from implementing forgiveness in your life as much as I did.

19

Clearing Blockages And Opening The Heart

Exercises 1:

S it or stand up straight in a quiet space. Make sure your spine is erect, feet shoulders width apart if you are standing. If you are sitting, the hills of your feet touching, and the head is parallel to the Universe.

Send the grounding cord of light from the Solar Plexus to the core of Mother Earth. We ground our physicality the most by sending love and gratitude to Mother Earth and her crystal core in the center. Open to receive her love and blessings in return.

Take a few deep breaths through your central channel.

Visualize the silver crystalline beam of light, 3-6 inches wide, shining throughout the center of your whole body. The light is bringing in the higher frequencies of light from Earth below and the Cosmos above.

Both streams of crystalline light-frequency are saturating in the middle of your chest and the heart, emitting a brilliant light.

Grounded and centered, feel your presence. Looking from above, observe and embrace all the feelings and emotions within you, for a few minutes, without judgment.

Stay with the feelings and emotions that are coming up, even if it feels uncomfortable. Observe, with no attachment, what is happening within you. The team is, we observe to know ourselves. To observe all the states of consciousness that pass through our awareness is being on the path of awareness. **Therefore, to observe and love all states and aspects of ourselves is the beginning of the awakening process.**

Knowing that love can heal, prevents sickness, rejuvenates and prolong our lives, send love and appreciation to all occasions, emotional and mental images that are arising within you.

As we observe ourselves, through the hear, we experience full heart awakening, the unification, and love with the moment, then the heart opens more to those changes that free painful memories.

Also, self-observation and reflection, with love and acceptance, align us with our higher-self aspects that are unconditional and limitless in every way.

In the stillness of the mind and openness of our higher-self heart, we access our heart's intelligence. Thus, through this knowingness in stillness, we expand within in sovereignty and integrity.

When we listen to the messages of our higher-self presence, they unite us within and with the outer world, Thus, united and liberated, we flow freely and eternally in the here and now.

Consequently, all unnecessary themes, emotions, and feelings are released in this perfection of love and stillness of the heart.

For example, we heal the feelings of fear or lack through

our higher self's love and light. For one, we are preventing the accumulation of negative memories in our consciousness and subconsciousness through this higher self's presence awareness.

Secondly, we are liberating our lives day by day through the process of self-love, acceptance, and the perfection of higher-self love.

Subsequently, through this process, we are uniting with our higher-self aspects.

Gradually, through self-reflection in stillness, we move to a space beyond the physical and into the embodiment and light of our higher self's presence.

Observing Like An Ascended Master

When we are one with our Higher Self's presence, through the portal of the heart in the now, all that we seek can unfold within us.

Therefore, send love and light to all beings, things, and the issues that came up. Namely, use this time to deepen the aspects and feelings inside.

So, go deeper embrace the intensity of any pain from the present, past, and future through the higher self divine love.

Know that the pain is also a springboard to the new beginning and the new you. Be excited about your rebirth through releasing the painful experiences and ending resistance to your expanded self through love.

Trust the process, let the smaller self dissolve into the higher self lead to the reigns of our liberation from oppression. Being and living the union within, through the heart in love and compassion, is the alchemy we all desire.

Besides, in harmony and unity within, all aspects of life are joined as one.

When you feel that you completed the self-observation and reflection for that day, affirm silently or aloud for a few minutes:

I open my heart to receive all the blessings from this abundant Universe.

In the end, thank your heart and soul for their cooperation and healing you received.

You can repeat this exercise anytime and when you feel there is a resistance within any aspect of you. Also, you can benefit from heart-opening reflection meditation anytime you have a moment of peace.

Exercise 2:

One Heart Consciousness Meditation

Sit or stand up straight in an upright position. Be sure your spine is straight, feet shoulders width apart, if you are standing. If sitting, the hills of your feet touching and head parallel to the Universe.

Send the grounding silver string of light from the solar plexus area through the center of the body to the core of Mother Earth. Visualize the crystalline light coming from Earth's center, creating the tube of luminous light going through your central channel and away up to the Universe. Imagine crystalline light is coming back down through the top of the head and accumulating in the middle of the chest, forming the vortex of crystalline green dazzling light.

The light carries the emanation of your talents and abilities, and its translucent green tone harmonizes and amplifies their potency within you. Take a few deep breaths of light-frequencies coming from Mother Earth, and the Universe, boosting the light and potential power of your heart-center.

Stay in this space of radiating and emitting your traits to the world freely and fully through your auric field. Open yourself to receive the blessings and love back from all the beings you have touched. See, your aura is feeling up with the crystalline particles of your gifts and offers, creating a blanket of shimmering translucent grass green light around you. This light is attracting your highest destiny and purpose.

Now, imagine the rose pink color overtaking the green, creating the emanation of crystalline rose-pink light of your higher heart. The unconditional love for others and self is now emanating from the center of your chest to all beings. Your Higher Self love is manifesting through all you are, and the whole body is emitting the rose-pink crystalline raise of unconditional love to all around.

Stay for a few minutes in this state of your higher consciousness to receive the cosmic, universal, the Divine Source, and your higher-self love for all that you are.

Receive the nourishment for a few more minutes.

Now, move the focus up a little bit and towards the middle of the upper chest. Visualize the fluorescent crystalline turquoise light saturating your upper chest.

See the turquoise light expanding recalling the fluid nature of your One Heart residing here.

Visualize the oceans and the seas of Earth subdividing in your One Heart, purifying and connecting your consciousness with all consciousness, and creating one expanded crystalline translucent One-Heart field.

So, as the oceans and waters serve everyone equally with humility, resilience, and vigor, as is your One Heart,

emitting diamond raise of crystalline light to all beings.
Your One Heart is leading the way to the unconditional life in sovereignty, integrity, and freedom for all.

Now, see the birds of the oceans subdividing their wings within your shoulder blades, creating crystalline wings of the One Heart. Feel, your one-heart crystalline wings brushing of and igniting the flight and liberation for you and many others.
Stay with this visualization of your One Heart opulence and expand it at least eleven feet all around you. See and feel the scope of your One Heart emitting the light away beyond your field.

As you feel comfortable with it, visualize the translucent crystalline turquoise light expanding and uniting the consciousness of people around you and beyond. You can stay with this visualization and listen to your heart and soul for the unique guidance for your One Heart exploration.

We all have different tasks to fulfill, and the One Heart meditation can be a unique journey for everyone. Therefore, allow yourself to relax into visualizing a crystalline turquoise diamond light emanating from all beings and things.
Continue to visualize the awakening of more people to One Heart consciousness and awareness. Thus, bringing unity and higher dimensions of consciousness to the New Earth and all beings.

20

Connecting To The Essence Within

Exercise 1:

Three Steps And Guidance For Overcoming Challenges

When we experience challenges in any aspect of our lives, we can be sure that our physical and spiritual worlds are not in harmony. The physical world, and the way we experience it, it is not in balance with our innate nature. In other words, our outer world, the Yang, is not harmonized with our inner world, the Yin.

It is simple, although it seems complicated at the time of difficulty.

For this reason, let us recall the Universal principle and law of Yin and Yang and how we can implement it for the issues we sometimes experience.

Everything has Yin and Yang. Therefore any aspect of life has it, too:

When Yin and Yang are in balance, we experience harmony. In the state of harmony for the aspect of life, also, there is no room for a challenge to manifest.

In this chapter, I will explain the technique that implements the wisdom of the yin and yang principle and law in combination with the soul power teachings, for overcoming obstacles.

The following three simple steps can help us avoid most of the problems and can ease the way of making important decisions. Let me explain further the soul wisdom behind this technique.

The Universal Law Of Yin And Yang Relating To Our Challenges

Generally speaking, Universal law means something that can be applied to everything, universally. Yin stands for many things in life, and in this instance, it means our innate nature.

Thus, regarding an issue we experience, Yin is the inner world within us.

Similarly, Yang, among many meanings also, means physical, a challenge or the outside world, in this case.
So, we want to bring our inner world in alignment with the outer world, to avoid obstacles in life.

Therefore, by implementing the Yin and Yang principle and law, we can create the balance, harmony, and flow within our troubled aspect.

We apply three easy steps.

Step 1: Identify the challenge.

In other words, we acknowledge and face the physical aspect of the issue and what it is.

To identify the issue is an easy step since our problem has already manifested.

Step 2: In the morning, when we first wake up, when our mind is peaceful, clear, and receptive, with less or no chatter, we connect to our Yin aspect of this trouble.

We connect to our inner world reality and the nature-- the soul of this issue. Exactly, we invoke the power of our soul through the heart center to identify the root cause.

Our soul, the light being within, is always ready and willing to assist us. All we need to do is to ask for assistance and tune in to listen for the guidance.

An Invocation To Our Soul And The Higher Self

Say Hello, as we would to a friend on the street.

Dear my beloved soul, I love you, please offer me an understanding and guidance on how I can transform my _____ situation, or finances, my anger, my resistance, my relationship, my health challenge __, or any one thing at the time, we want to resolve.

We elaborate in detail, our problem, and the help we seek. Talk to your innate being like you would to a friend, family member, or a psychologist.

At the end of our inquire, we say Thank You, to our soul in sincere appreciation.

The more our heart is open, and the more we are honestly expressing our need, the more we will obtain the appropriate answers.

Our soul has all the knowledge, experience, wisdom, and answers we will ever need. We talk to our soul like we would to a very close friend.

When we finish with addressing the issue, we quiet down and listen to the messages that our soul has for us. At this point, the trust and faith that we can hear the answer are important. This takes practice and being easy on yourself.

Even if you cannot hear anything, at first, all you need to do is send more love to your soul and trust.

The key to this communication and contemplation is patients in the feelings of vastness, love, and gratitude. Repeat the process until you completely become one with it. In other words, you become a patient and an open-hearted listener of your higher self being.

Give it some time in loving support, imagining golden light in the area between your physical heart and the heart chakra, where the Soul Temple is.

Visualizing the golden sphere of light in this area of the Soul Temple in the middle of the chest, just to the left of the Heart Chakra. Consciously connecting to our heart center will assure that the guidance we receive is in alignment with our highest purpose and plan.

Trust And Follow Up On Guidance You Received

Additionally, be mindful not to have many expectations, since these messages are very subtle and delicate, so any of our attitudes or big expectations may dissolve the messages and push them away.

Finally, if the answer does not come right then, we have to know that the answer will come in different ways sometimes later. We can receive the message in the form of image, word, sentence, or just an inner knowingness of the answer anytime later.

Therefore, the point is to ask and to be aware that the guidance is coming, thus to trust our soul and be aware.

Sometimes we may be guided to an event, newspaper, to an action that will reveal some answers and guidance for our inquire.
Additionally, we can re-phrase the question at another time to receive more information and what we need to know.

Step 3: Step three is the most important that is to follow the guidance we receive from our soul.

Balancing The Inner With the Outer World Can Heal Our Challenges

In its essence, what we want is to pay respect to our souls' wants and needs. We do NOT want to make decisions that are solely guided by our minds and common knowledge.

So, our physical lives, no matter how good or bad they look and feel like, at the time, if they are not aligned with our innate true nature, and our soul desires, they will not be beneficial to us; in the long run, we are bound to experience challenges and difficulties. Our unhappy Soul will create and attract problems and challenges for us to experience, and to learn lessons.

Real-life Experience And Teaching

Let me illustrate with a practical example, I have experienced in my life.

In 2006, I joined the venture, in order 'just to make money' to support my physical life and soul journey. I was aware that joining this venture is not aligned with my highest soul's potential, and purpose.
I failed to obey my soul's messages.

I joined the venture since my powerful mind, at that time, believed it can play it off and trick my spirit and the soul, and come back to it when I meet my immediate needs. The truth is I ended up having a draining and depleting time for over 6-7 years. I had invested much time and money, and have not accomplished my goal of reaching financial freedom.

On the contrary, I ended up in massive debt and exhausted I left the venture at the end of 2012.
I have to stop right here, although this was not the end of my financial downfall.

My example may seem very drastic and to the extreme to you, but I can assure you that the more powerful your soul is, the more challenges it can create for you to experience and learn lessons.

Final Words On Overcoming Challenges

It is my sincere desire that something like this does not happen to you, my beloved readers. That is why I have enclosed the simple advice and method to help you avoid a similar discord in your life.

You can apply the 3-step technique for overcoming challenges through implementing the yin and yang principle and your soul power to any area or an aspect of life.
Essentially, our innate light being and the Higher Self can help us solve the problems in our relationships, finances, decision makings, or otherwise.
You can be confident in this truth.

"Ask (in this instance your soul) and it shall be given to you." That is what the Bible says, and so it is.

WENG

YOU
HONG

HEI

Body's Soul Channel

Exercise 2:

Soul Channel Activation

Our Soul Channel can be activated by connecting and visualizing light between the Crown Chakra, the First Chakra, Third Chakra, and the acupuncture point, across from the navel to the back. Please refer to the illustration on previous page 160. Consequently, the visualization is two ellipses crossing in the area of the navel.

The sounds that resonate and vibrate these energy centers creating the Soul Channel in a body are:

Weng (pronounced wong)– the 7th Chakra–Crown chakra–very top of the head

Hei (pronounced as hey)– the 1st Chakra–Root chakra– at the bottom of the torsos

Hong (pronounced hong) – the 3rd Chakra–Solar plexus area–the navel area

You (pronounced yo:)– the acupuncture point, straight across from navel to the back.
Invoke your Soul Channel first, before you start the practice. Invocation to the inner world:

Dear soul, mind, and body of my Soul Channel, I love you, you have the power to activate fully, align me with my original message, and bring my soul abilities and potential to life. Do a good job. Thank you.

Connect also, to the outer world for assistance and boost. Invocation (outer world):

Dear Divine, the Source, and countless planets, stars, galaxies, and universes, I love you. You have the power to boost the potential power of my Soul. Thank you.

Chant or sing 5-10 minutes at a time while visualizing the crystalline white or golden light rings circling and connecting the appointed energy centers in the body: Weng (Wong), Hei (hey), Hong,You (yo:).Repeat the sounds until you go into a condition of being connected and one within and with all that is.

In Conclusion On Soul Channel Practice

We are all transmitters of frequency and vibration of our consciousness in a form. When we are in a conscious state of harmony and content, we acknowledge and transmit our united field of awareness through the universe and others.

We receive from the holographic feedback loop of the universe what we put out. Therefore, our effort to unite within, through our higher state of light consciousness, plays a vital role and benefit all beings.

As a transmitter of higher frequency of light, we excel and assist more people to awake and to be aware, thus, the higher frequency of the light is available to everyone.

At this monumental time of our acceleration, we have the opportunity, to succeed in our realization, unification, and ascension process, within and with the outer world.

By connecting firmly to our essence within and the higher levels of consciousness through activating the Soul Channel of the body, we can awaken more of the potential power of our soul and be the vehicles of the higher frequency of light consciousness of our soul here and now.

21

Grounding In Love And Light To Healing Negative Memories

Grounding In Love And Light To Healing

L et me introduce the soul power wisdom and practice to ground ourselves in love and light.

The lower abdomen is the second most significant part of the body, where our power resides, besides the heart center, Additionally, the lower abdomen is equally significant for our well-being, longevity, and transformation journey.

The whole sphere below the navel, in between the 1st and 3rd Chakras, and to the back-spinal cord and tailbone area, create our body foundational energy.

This whole space in the lower abdomen is the engine of our physical body, significantly influencing our might and well-being. Thus, the area of the lower abdomen is where our energy, stamina, vitality, and immunity are produced and stored.

Also, this very foundational energy center of our body through the spinal cord and central nervous system effects and supports our mind and brain functionality.

Therefore, in the ancient teachings, such as Buddhist, Hindu, and more, this area is the second most important area to develop for acceleration on all levels of life.

Exercise 1:

Firstly, bring the focus to the lower abdomen, taking a few deep breaths to the space couple of inches below the navel. Take a full breath through your nose, and exhale through the mouth. Feel your lower abdomen expanding gently on the inhale and subsiding on the slow exhale.

Visualize, now a golden ball of light, spinning count-clockwise in this foundation of your body, while radiating and emitting golden rays of light throughout the body. The light is connecting you to the core of the earth.

Repeat an inhale, and an exhale in this way by visualizing the golden light ball radiating for a few more breaths. Feel the light spreading out and receiving the nourishment from the Earth, as well as from the Universe above.

Send the grounding cord from the navel to the core of the earth and see it coming back, through your central channel away above.
Repeat silently or aloud:

I am light, I am love, I am a channel of love and light for the Universe.

Mother Earth is nourishing me with her love and light.

I am open to receive all the blessings that are available to me, now.

Firstly, experience love, light, and gratitude coming up to your lower abdomen and from there permeate your whole being. Mother Earth is nourishing you with her love and light.

Receive the shower of brilliant white light coming down through the Crown Chakra and your auric field from the Universe above. In this state, repeat the invocations for a few minutes.

The wisdom is that the more we are grounded in love and gratitude to planet earth, the more we open, and the higher frequencies of the light and consciousness we can experience and receive from the Universe.

What is more significant, when we consciously shift our focus and energy to our foundation as opposed to the mind and being in the head, through thought patterns, we experience peace and contentment.
The more we practice bringing the energy to our foundation, the more we can feel grounded and liberated.

Practice by repeating affirmations and visualizing light in your lower abdomen. Now, expend the light out through the body's auric field and beyond for 3-10 minutes. Through visualization, bring strength in love and gratitude to your body and all beings.

This ancient method and wisdom can quickly lift much darkness from our souls, hearts, and minds at any time, especially at challenging times.

Developing Foundational Energy Center

As stated, the body's foundation is in the lower abdomen. The lower abdomen is a storehouse of our energy, stamina, virility, and immunity.
When we develop a strong foundation, our energy, stamina,

vitality, and immunity increase as a result, we are prolonging our lives, also.
To illustrate, think of a tree.

The trees have a root that is going deep into the ground as deep as their height. Therefore, threes have away longer lives than humans.
Also, an even better example is a house or building. What is a house without a good foundation?

The exercise to develop a strong foundation takes 10-15 minutes per time, and we can do them anytime and anywhere. They are simple and we can work on developing our foundational energy on the bus, subway while commuting to work while walking, or anytime we have a few minutes at hand.

It is good to know, with a strong foundation we can have a better quality of life by a hundred times fold.

In the ancient teachings, including Traditional Chinese Medicine, Foundational energy centers of the body are:

• Lower Dan Tian (about 1" below the navel, and 1.5" inside the body; visualize a fist size golden ball)

• Kundalini is the second major foundational energy center, located in front of the tail bone and 1.5" inside the body; visualize the fist-size golden ball.
Both foundational energy centers are the key to long life. Thus, if you desire to live long or longer, a strong foundation for your physical body is necessary.

Additionally, Kundalini is the energy center that determines the quality of our lives; it nourishes the kidneys, also provides food for the brain and the Third Eye.
The Third Eye is a cherry-size energy center, in the middle of the brain, facilitating our intuition, telepathy, and

advanced spiritual abilities such seeing images beyond the physical realm.

A strong foundation can support the development of all other energy centers, such as the heart, our speech—the vocal expression, brain abilities, and more.

Having a solid trunk—a good foundation of our body also brings inner peace and mental clarity.
Considering the many benefits of developing the foundation of our physical bodies, I can foresee the foundational energy practices soon to be taught in primary schools.

Living its benefits, I believe the development of the body's foundation is important 10-15 minutes per day practice to increase our productivity, energy, vitality, immunity, and overall health.

Fifteen minutes each day is the minimum time needed to develop a foundation. Usually, it is better to do it two times for 5-10 minutes per day. The first thing in the morning and later on in the day would be more appropriate for the beginning.

Now that we know where the foundational energy center is and its main benefits, I will introduce the simplest technique that can promote health for all generations, from children to adults and elders, respectively.

Bring in the Light of the Universe to Your Foundation

Visualize golden Light satiating your trunk and accumulating sun's energy and light-force into your lower abdomen.

See and feel, the light is creating a golden light-ball in both areas, the lower Dan Tian, just below the navel, and the front of the tailbone, Kundalini area.

This is a great daily visualization when we first wake up or any time.

One of the essential pieces of wisdom for developing the foundation of our physical form is refocusing the energy and attention, at all times, from a busy head to where is needed in the lower abdomen, the center of our energy, stamina, vitality, and immunity, boosting our life's force.

Therefore, visualize the golden light balls in your lower abdomen expanding and emitting light from this center to the whole body. Stay with this visualization for some minutes and anytime during the day.

The wisdom is, instead of the intention and focus leaking all over the body and through redundant thoughts, we focus it here in the core and distribute it from this one place to the whole body.

Imagine the engine of the car.

Even just visualizing the golden light in these areas, below the navel, and in front of the tailbone, creating the sphere of light while performing daily activities can be very beneficial to your well-being.

Firstly, by refocusing attention and focus, we train our minds to be focused, relaxed, calm, and in a meditative state, when we are more productive, too.

The second benefit of developing a good foundation is that our energy, vitality, stamina, and immunity to physical illness increases. As well as mental and emotional challenges lessen.

Indeed, the ancients knew well how to increase energy and vitality naturally through visualization, focused intention, and repeating wisdom words.

Exercise 2:

To boost the development of our foundation, we can add sound and soul power to a visualization of the golden balls.

The sound that vibrates the lower abdomen area below the naval is 'joe' (pronounced jo:).

The sound that vibrates the Kundalini area, infant of the tailbone, is 'yi' (pronounced yi:).

The Soul Power is the invocation to the soul of our foundational energy and giving it love and appreciation with a commend to develop fully.

I will explain the Soul Orders technique in more detail in Chapter 24. For now, we can give a commend to any part of our body, mind, and spirit to heal or transform. It sounds like this:

"Dear soul, mind, and body of my foundational energy centers, the Lower Dan Tian, and Kundalini. I love you. You have the power to develop fully and boost my energy, stamina, vitality, and immunity.
Do a good job. Thank you."

It is beneficial to put your hands just below the navel one palm over the other, or grab the left-hand thumb with the right hand and let the left-hand fingers resting around the fist of the right hand.

This hand position is called the Yin/Yang palm position, effective for developing a strong foundation and balancing the body's Yin and Yang at the same time.

Logically, where we put the hands is where the energy and light go. So, in this practice we put both hands over the lower abdomen below the navel or one hand below the navel and the other on Kundalini on the tail bone area.

At this time, repeat for 5-10 minutes at a time, the sounds that vibrate these two areas: 'joe' and 'yi' while visualizing the golden light radiating and expanding in your foundation, the Lower Abdomen, and Kundalini area in front of the tail-bone.

22

Breathing Techniques

The Ancient Yogic Breathing Technique Explained

T he following breathing techniques we can do while sitting in the meditative position in the chair, on the floor, or on the ground. Additionally, try them as well as while standing or walking and doing other day-to-day activities.

I believe if we do it more offend is a significant point for being connected within and a faster acceleration at this time of rapid changes.
When the technique becomes second nature to us, we can uplift our spirit' in this way anytime.

Through breath and breathing, we can experience the Now moment, fully. All that we have for certain is only the now. Therefore, there is nothing more potent than experiencing Heaven on Earth through the heart-breath in the now moment.

When we observe our breath and all thoughts and emotions that arise within us, through the eyes of wonder, love, and being fully present, we are gradually aligning with our Higher Self presence in every moment.

The Tantric Breath Technique

We start with an exhale first to oxygenate our bodies the most; take a breath through the mouth and let it fill up your belly firstly by making the sound of the ocean wave rising.

Secondly, let the breath flow up naturally, filling the rib-cage and the chest. With breath rising, the chest and the spine are lengthening and shoulders are expanding outwards, also naturally. Once the breath reaches the throat area, we can experience the lengthening of the neck and raising of the head up, a bit, naturally, where it stops in the back of the throat for few moments, and just before a slow exhale, making that beautiful sound of the ocean wave falling--the feeling of release. The exhale will make the chin slightly tucked down, and shoulders pushed outwards, with the spine still expended, and throughout the full exhale.

Although it seems like a three steps breath, it is to be one long wave of breath, without stops. There is only one stop for a moment when breath reaches the back of the throat, and just before the exhale.
Try this now for few consequent rounds of exhaling and inhaling by visualizing beautiful waves of white crystalline light moving through you.

The suggested minimum for experiencing an immediate benefit is taking the six rounds of breath at the time. Immediately you can notice all of your cells vibrating, contracting, and expanding harmoniously.

The Alternation of Tantric Breathing Through the Nostrils

We can use another variation of this original Tantric yogic breathing technique, with the alternate holding of either nostril while inhaling and exhaling.

Inhale through the left nostril, while using the thumb to close the right nostrils, hold the breath in the middle of the head for few seconds, and on the exhale, use the middle finger to close the left nostrils while exhaling out through the right nostrils. Now, take the breath through the right nostril you have just exhaled, and repeat the process for a minimum of six rounds.

Try it now by adding the count of six bits while the inhale through one nostril while closing the opposite nostril with one finger, hold the breath in the head for six counts, and exhale out through the opposite nostril while releasing the finger, through counts of six bits. Now, take the breath with the same nostril you have just exhaled by holding the opposite one for six counts and repeat the process. for six rounds at a time.

Consequently, through this alternating nostrils breathing, we are bringing the light force of the Universe to the middle of the head that is harmonizing the left and right brain hemispheres. Besides the immediate calming sensation within our busy brain and mind, it stimulates the Third Eye and our intuitive abilities. Also. I found this technique very handy for quickly obtaining peace in the middle of a busy day. Try it, to experience is to believe.

The Extended Tantric Breath Technique Using Locks

The second—and an extended part of the same breathing exercise will awaken our central channel, all seven, and twelve Chakras will be on fire. Furthermore, the extended practice will assist us in experiencing the perfect Bliss and One Heart consciousness with everyone and everything, In other words, the heightened awareness of being one within and with everything.

Through some practice ,we can go beyond this time and space, the experience of Samadhi or the perfect Bliss. Like the ancient yogic masters, yet right here and now, and wherever we are on earth, due to the higher frequencies of light available everywhere.

For the extended breathing practice, we will do the same steps of the Tantric breathing and will just add '3 locks' for each part of the one complete round of breath.
Let us begin:

The 1st lock

Start with the exhale and then take the breath through the mouth, filling up the belly first, at that moment we gently contract the anus (muscle right above the perineum). This is our 1st lock.

Notice an extra push to our breath, and lengthening of the abdomen and of the rib cage after the 1st lock. Thus the spine is extending with shoulders opening outwards and up.

The 2nd Lock

After filling up the belly and when the breath passes the shoulder blades, we are to implement the 2nd lock in the area between the shoulder blades that will fill and stretch the chest outwards and up more. Consequently, it will also push the air and light up vigorously to the back of the throat.

The 3rd Lock

When the breath reaches the back of the throat with a stop for a few moments, , we are to apply the 3rd lock just before the slow exhale through the mouth. Let the sound of exhaling freely out by visualizing the ocean wave falling. While tacking the chin down a bit and pushing out the breath, with the spine and shoulders being stretched up and outwards, through the full exhale.

This is all happening naturally, not involving much effort on our part, we are just executing the natural movement of the breath through our system.

Try it now, for the full six rounds of breath to experience it.

Implementing the locks serve as an extra push to the light throughout our focused, conscious breathing.

It is noticeable that the locks are the pump to push the air and the light easily and naturally through body.

Through visualization, the 1st lock can be a signal that we light up all the chakra energy vortexes and to feel the surge of energy and light coming up the central channel.

The light, throughout our body is awakening all cells, and it is moving up through the crown to the Universe expanding our consciousness with each breath.

Consequently, all the parts of the body receive a message and strengthen and expand in frequency and light through each round of conscious breath.

Be creative with visualization and activation of your chakras and the light through your body. You can do everyday different visualization by reconnecting different chakras, and make various intentions every time you practice.

23

Developing Compassion For Our Life And The Lives Of Others

T he Soul Power Techniques we use for transformation or healing of any aspect of life.

For example, in Soul Power teachings and knowledge, the experience and feeling of compassion boost energy, stamina, vitality, and immunity.

If you have not recognized this wisdom in your life, I suggest that you experience it today.

To do so, bring to your mind the occasion when you experienced compassion while the event, for a person, a group, or at any time you felt an extensive feeling of compassion or empathy for something.

If you bring that occasion to your heart, now I am sure you can feel your energy rising from within, and your heart is warming and opening wider.

Also, if it was a sincere feeling of compassion, you can feel resilience and fortitude growing within you, even today.

In other words, you feel empowered and invigorated just by recalling the event you felt and experienced compassion for someone or something.

The compassion for others and oneself are a perfect example of the benefits we can receive by offering these great qualities of love and compassion to others, and our lives.

Additionally, there is a powerful example of an unconditional saint servant, I benefited greatly from, who can assist us in growing the compassion of our hearts and souls. Her name is Guan Yin, the bodhisattva of compassion and mercy.

Guan Yin, in her lifetime on earth, gave the vow to humanity and the Divine to assist anyone who calls her name when experiencing difficulty or danger.
Exactly when her teacher introduced her to The Greatest Compassion Mantra, she gave the vow to serve humanity and spread her compassion and the mantra through all her lives.

Since then, there are many stories, throughout history, of people drowning or in danger calling her name, and her soul would come and save their lives.

You do not need to be in a life-threatening event to experience Guan Yin's unconditional servant soul and offerings.

For example, when you are in disharmony, also when you are developing your compassion, invite Guan Yin soul to bless you. You will feel her love, compassion, and uplift to an occasion.

Let me now lead you through the soul power technique for developing and increasing our compassion.

As always, we start with the invocation and invite the inner souls first. In this instance, the soul of our heart, and our ability to instigate and generate feelings of compassion. Everything has a soul, as well as the consciousness (mind), and physical existence (the manifestation).

Therefore, the invocation would sound like this:

Dear soul, mind, and body of my heart and soul. I love you. You have the power to flourish through developing and expanding my compassion in my life and my soul journey. Do a good job! Thank you.

Then we invite the outer souls, for example, the soul of Guan Yin or the Divine, the Universe, cosmos, whoever means the higher power for you.

For example:

Dear soul, mind, and body of Guan Yin, the bodhisattva of compassion, I love you. Please, bless me to expand the capacity of my heart to experience compassion so that I can be happier and healthier. I am very grateful. Thank you.

Now, recite, sing, or chant for 3-10 minutes at a time:

The *Greatest Compassion is filling my heart and soul, and my life is blooming with happiness and joy. Guan Yin is blessing my request.*

Thank you, Guan Yin. Thank you, my soul. I am very grateful.

The example is an instance of the soul power technique to self-heal and transforms any characteristic or an aspect of our lives.

To recap on the wisdom behind the practice, remembering that everything has a soul, the soul has the power to heal, and when the soul heals, the transformation on the physical plane follows.

Therefore, the invocation consists of five parts:

1. We invoke the soul of the aspect or anything we wish to transform or heal.

2. Express love and thank the soul we invoked in advance.

3. State and request for healing or transformation.

4. Express gratitude in advance.

5. Start singing or reciting your request in absolute love and recognition for 3-10 minutes at a time, forgetting about the request but going into the feeling nature of the request.

There are no time limits in practicing and expanding our compassion, any aspect, or self-healing an issue.
The more we go into a condition of love, appreciation, and surrender to the task, and our devotion, the more benefits we can receive for our request.
In other words, after finishing the invocation, do not think about your immediate needs and activities, while reciting and visualizing. Complete surrender and go into a condition of openness and oneness with the Source and the vastness of the Universe to receive the unfolding of your request.
Try it now to surrender while utilizing this self-healing technique, it takes a little bit of practice and our trust in the process.

Usually, both surrender and trust come with practicing more often and receiving benefits.
Be creative and change the quality of compassion to another aspect you want to develop, transform, or heal.
I wish you could benefit from these simple soul power techniques for healing and transformation, as much as I did.

Additionally, in the same way, with this five-step technique and modified invocations, we can request the healing of any impairment within our physical, mental, emotional, and spiritual bodies.

As you may notice, the possibilities of the soul power techniques for self-healing and transformation are endless, because everything has a soul, the mind (consciousness), and the body (existence). Naturally, we can invoke any of our souls, or the souls of different aspects of our lives, for healing and transformation in the same way.

More soul power wisdom, techniques, and ideas on how to implement them are in the following Chapters.

24

The Soul Orders
For Healing, Transformation,
Acceleration, & Rejuvenation

Now, I will share the technique I learned while studying Soul Healing and Enlightenment that assisted me extensively in my healing, purification, acceleration, and awakening journey.

Implementation and many variations of the following wisdom and technique can help you achieve your goals and heart's desires more quickly.

It is so simple that you may think I can't believe that this can heal, impact, and change my life.

Know that the simplest things are the most profound and life-changing. There is an ancient saying that resonates with this truth:

The Big Way Is Extremely Simple.

So, I suggest that you pay attention, as this self-healing method can move your healing, transformation, and acceleration process to a different level.

The method also proceeds from the Soul Power wisdom and knowledge that everything has a soul and the soul has the power to heal.

All the inanimate and animate things and beings have souls, including our organs, systems, cells, nucleolus, protons, and tiniest matter they have souls.

Similarly, any aspect of life, such as our health, finances, and relationships they have a soul, too.

There are also outer souls of the Divine, the Source, our spiritual fathers and mothers, holy beings, lamas, gurus, Buddha's, Bodhisattvas, healing angels, archangels, and more they have the soul and can assist the healing and transformation process.

Additionally, which is the crux of this technique is that we can give an order to our soul and souls of anything regarding and concerning our lives, and us directly.

Therefore, the method is called Soul Orders.

Also, it is essential to know and keep in mind, we can not give an order for healing or transformation to the soul of others and their concerns.

On the contrary, we would create negative consequences or karma by interfering with any person's soul, without their permission.

Naturally, this is the spiritual law that we do not want to break to benefit.

So, the following technique is for your use to transform, heal, and benefit your life.

Of course, you can always do a forgiveness practice, sing mantras for others to evolve, and do Soul Healing techniques by omitting Soul Orders (as the one in the previous Chapter).

The following invocation is the Soul Order for your healing, transformation, and any of your concerns.

We invoke the soul of anything we have an issue with and send an order for transformation or healing.

It is also a five-step process:

1. First, we invoke the soul of an issue/challenge you are experiencing.

2. Give love to it.

3. Send the order for healing or transformation

4. Express appreciation from your heart by thanking the souls in advance.

5. Repeat the order three times with conviction.

If time allows, repeat it for additional 3-5 minutes at a time. For instance, if you were heaving a health challenge with your liver, for example, the invocation would sound like this.

Dear my body soul. I love you. Give an order to the soul, mind, and body of my liver to heal and rejuvenate completely. Thank you.

Then you activate the order:

My body soul orders my liver to heal and rejuvenate completely. Thank you.

or

Dear soul, mind, and body of my liver. I love you, honor you, and appreciate you.

Heal and rejuvenate completely. Do a good job.

Thank you.

Then you activate the order:

The soul order to my liver: Heal and rejuvenate yourself. Do a good job. Thank you.

The last step is to repeat the order for three times with conviction.

If times allows you can repeat an order for 3-5 minutes at a time or longer there is no time limit.

As always if we want to boost our invocation, we can invite the outer soul of the Divine, the Source, or any of your spirit guides, saints, ascended masters, or angels, any holy being you feel connected to.

Dear Divine, I love you. Please, heal and rejuvenate my liver. I am very grateful, Thank you.

After we invoked the inner and outer souls, repeated the order for three times, we can continue singing or chanting while visualizing a golden light, in the area of the organ or an aspect in challenge.

For this example, visualize a bright golden or green florescent sphere of light emanating from your liver. Repeat:

My liver is healed and rejuvenated completely. Thank you.
Divine is healing and blessing my liver. Thank you, Divine.

If you have a chronic condition, you need to repeat and visualize the light in the area of your organ or an aspect in a challenge, for up to two hours per day to experience benefits.

You can also do a few 15 minutes practices to add time to two hours or more per day.

Go into a condition of love and surrender to the light, the Divine, the Source, your soul, and keep practicing.

You can be amazed at the progress you experience in your whole body. The healing will take place not only in your physical condition but will rejuvenate your mind, emotions, and your spiritual body, also.

If you would like to assure you are receiving the most of this self-healing method, you can add a short Forgiveness practice (Chapter 18) concerning your issue, before the soul order.

Similarly, if you are suffering from fear or you have any emotional, mental, or spiritual conditions you wish to transform you can send an order to the soul of your fear, for example as follows.

The soul order to my fear: Heal and transform yourself into calmness and content. Do a good job. Thank you.

or

My body soul orders my fear to heal and transform into peace and content. Thank you.

Repeat the order three times with a conviction or repeat the soul other for 3-5 minutes at a time.

25

Physical Existence — The Matter Transformation To Light

Advancing The Body's Matter, To Energy, Energy To Message, Message To Emptiness & Emptiness To The Light

B y transforming the body's matter to the light within our physical form, the heart, mind, or spirit, we are raising our body's frequency and moving into a more ethereal form. Additionally, removing dense entities from our character or any aspect of life can advance our lives on all levels of being.

In Chapter 13 on the Enlightenment journey, I mentioned the following technique used to transform the physical to the higher frequency light and form.

Therefore, proceeding with Taoist practice, we can use to transform the challenges that are essentially the dense matter within our system to the lighter matter or light.

I included this Ancient wisdom and method in the

practical techniques since I believe it is profound to know about and its multiple implementations for our well-being.

In its essence, it is a transformation of physical or the matter, matter to energy, the energy to message, message to emptiness, an emptiness to the source is the evolving of the matter or any existence, to the lighter form and the lighter existence, eventually into the light frequency.

Naturally, the light can be the original Soul or the Source within us.

In the scoop, it is the process of creation and transformation of:

– the matter is created in the Kidneys;

– matter is transformed to energy, on the pathway from the base of the spine to the head.

- the energy transmutes to message– in our heads or the brain;

– the message evolves to emptiness, on the pathway from the brain to the heart

- and the final stage is the emptiness is transformed to the light (the Source) in the Heart Chakra

Consequently, the technique consists of a repetition of five phases with visualization.

– **First phase** is the creation of matter in the kidneys. The invocation is: *'Produce Matter'*

– **Second phase** is the matter transforms into energy in the spinal-cord.
'Transform Matter to Energy'

– **Third phase:** the energy is transforming to the message–in the brain.
'Transform Energy to Message'

ALTERING *the* Body's MATTER to *More* Ethereal FORM

TRANSFORMATION *of the* Body's *Matter to Light*

3. Energy Transforms
to Message (in the Brain)

4. Message Transforms
to Emptiness
(on the patway from
the head to the heart)

2. Matter Transforms
to Energy
(in the Spinal Cord)

5. Emptiness
Transforms
to Light
(between the heart
and Heart Chakra)

1. Kidneys Produce
Matter

–**Fourth phase:** the message is transformed into emptiness; on the way from the head to the area of our physical heart. The invocation is:

'Transform Message to Emptiness'

–**Fifth phase:** Emptiness is transformed into the Light in the area of Heart Chakra. Here, in the middle of the chest area, also called the Soul' Temple.

The invocation is:

'Transform Emptiness to the Source"

The essence of the method is to repeat the process, or the invocations of this process in five phases: the creation of the matter, the matter to energy, energy to the message, the message to emptiness, and the emptiness to the Light through visualization.

Therefore, through the invocations and visualization, we are refining and raising the frequency of our physical form, our organs, systems, cells, our DNA, and RNA and transmute them to a more pure, and higher frequency form.

As mentioned, it can be applied successfully to any aspect of life we wish to heal, transform and evolve. For example, the excess of fear, worry, insecurity, to boost confidence, and so on.

The exact way I learned how to practice while studying with the Institute of Soul Healing and Enlightenment is explained in the following paragraphs.

I believe you can find this practice beneficial for your healing, transformation, and enlightenment journey.

The Practice

Produce Matter phase one

Where we put our hands that is where the energy goes. Put both palms on your kidneys, in the lower back, and close your eyes

Inhale deeply and visualize the **golden light** vibrating in your kidneys.

Invoke silently one time only:

'Produce Matter.'

Then hold your breath while repeating silently four times:

'Produce Matter' X4 times

Then exhale while invoking silently for one time: 'Produce Matter'

Repeat this cycle additional six times, total of seven times.

Transform Matter to Energy phase two

Hands position: Put one palm right across from navel to the back, and the other palm over the last bone of your spinal cord, in the back of the neck. Close your eyes.

Inhale deeply and visualize **rainbow light** moving from your kidneys, down to the base of the spine, and moving up, through the spinal cord to the base of the neck.

Invoke silently one time only:

'Transform Matter to Energy'.

Then hold your breath while repeating silently four times:

'Transform Matter to Energy' – X4 times

Exhale while repeating silently one time:

'Transform Matter to Energy'

Repeat this cycle six times, a total of seven times.

Transform Energy to Message phase three

Hands position: Leave one palm in the back, right across from the navel, and the other palm over the Crown Chakra, over the top of the head. Close your eyes gently.

Inhale deeply and at the same time visualize **purple light** vibrating in your brain.

Invoke silently one time only:

'Transform Energy to Message'.

Then hold your breath while repeating silently four times:

"Transform Energy to Message'- X4 times

Exhale while invoking silently one time:

'Transform Energy to Message'

Repeat this cycle six times, a total of seven times.

Transform Message to Emptiness phase four

Leave one palm across from the navel in the back, and put the other palm over your physical heart. Close your eyes gently.

Inhale deeply and at the same time visualize **crystal light** vibrating in the Heart.

Invoke silently one time only:

'Transform Message to Emptiness'.

Then hold your breath while repeating silently four times:

'Transform Message to Emptiness'- X4 times

Exhale while chanting silently 1 time:

'Transform Message to Emptiness'

Repeat this cycle six times, a total of seven times.

Transform Emptiness to Light phase five (the Source, Original-Light)

Hands position: Leave one palm across from navel in the

back, and put the other palm just next to the Heart' Chakra in the middle of the chest (where our Soul Temple is located). Close your eyes gently.

Inhale deeply and at the same time visualize **crystalline golden light** vibrating in the area of our Soul Temple in the middle of the chest.

Invoke silently one time only:

'Transform Emptiness to the Source Light'.

Then hold your breath while repeating silently four times:

'Transform Emptiness to the Source' X4 times

Exhale while invoking silently one time:

'Transform Emptiness to Source Light.'

Repeat this cycle six times, a total of seven times.

Naturally, as I mentioned, through focused intention while invocations and visualization, we can evolve any challenge or issues to dissipate, lessen, or transform to the light frequency.

Be creative and imaginative. Among many benefits, this technique can bring peace and tranquility to our hearts and souls. You can feel very peaceful and content just after one full round of all five cycles.

***We can rotate the left or the right hand that is placed in the back, opposite from the navel while practicing, and after each full round of five phrases X7   times cycle invocations to balance our Yin/Yang simultaneously.

26

The Ascension Grid Activation Meditation

T he good news is that acceleration, awakening, and our collective ascension, on all levels, are prevalent in the well-organized flow of the cosmos. **The Ascension grid exists around and above Earth's atmosphere to help humanity in the process of our awakening and moving to the higher states of consciousness globally.** Planet Earth has a significant place in this global evolution process, and it must evolve to the higher dimensions of consciousness, together with countless planets, stars, galaxies, and universes.

Due to our human struggles, through pandemic and beyond upheavals, at this critical time, we are assisted by the Ascended Masters and other advanced light beings of the universe through this high-frequency light field.

Many people are perplexed and dumfound in the net of fear, separation, and restriction-based awareness. These boundaries have to resolve, and human consciousness must expand for us to evolve to the next levels. Therefore, the Ascension grid is here to assist this cosmic reset and further our evolution.

This perfect geometrical energy and light frequency grid is in place as a tool for our individual and collective healing and dismantling of the chains and lower frequencies of very present three-dimensional reality.

So, we can connect and activate this high-frequency field by sending our love and light to it. Once the grid is activated, it lights up while streaming down a high-frequency light to humanity and Mother Earth. Thus, removing darkness and awakening more people to the new reality.

Liberation To The Higher States Of Consciousness

As our human consciousness awakes and expands influenced by the higher frequency of light from the Ascension grid, the illusion artificially placed on human consciousness can disintegrate.

In other words, once the 'Maya' banishes, we can experience the new higher realms of consciousness and awareness. Consequently, our higher selves aspect can rise above the illusionary realm.

The idea is for our collective belief systems to liberate and expand that we can experience our higher-self presence and frequencies of the New Earth and its realm. Higher dimensions are aspects of consciousness. Also, the dimensions are worlds of existence.

So, when we remove confusion and set free from fear, separation, and ignorance collectively and individually, we can evolve. Thus, move through different dimensions of consciousness intentionally.

Then, through the heart center and our higher-self love, we

are limitless beings as our birthright. Therefore, by connecting to the Ascension grid, we institute and upgrade to a frequency and notion of our unlimited potential as a being and help others experience the same.

When we work with the Ascension grid daily, we can notice our frequency is accelerating. Consequently, we experience heightened awareness for shorter or longer periods. So as our frequency rises and consciousness expands, we can let go of old patterns and suppressed belief systems.

Utilizing The Ascension Light Field

Given that everything has a soul, we do not need to be in the groups to perform this global ascension acceleration practice.
All we have to do at the beginning of practice is to invite the souls of humanity and light workers around the globe to practice with us.

Exactly, we are to invite and visualize all of us around the globe practicing together and simultaneously sending love and light frequencies up to the Ascension grid.
Thus, activated this light energy field is streaming down the ascension frequency and light to humanity and Mother Earth.

The light is awakening people who are asleep and offering upgrades to everyone as appropriate and for the highest good.

Everything is in divine flow and intelligence of the universe, creating configurations and upgrades to all, as it is needed.

Connected and attuned to the Ascension grid and our higher-self presence and purpose through divine love and light in our hearts, we are sending our light up, activating the ascension light field, and receiving blessings for our life and others in return.

It is significant to know and integrate the light frequency Ascension field at this time.
We have a chance to access higher realms of consciousness and awareness and usher them to prevail on Earth as the new normal.

So, when we access this high-frequency matrix, individually or in groups, we dissolve the negative within and from the collective.
Here is an opportunity to help humanity evolve and to benefit and receive virtue for our journey. Yes, our journey is blessed, and we are uplifted on all levels when we offer universal service like this.

The Law Of Universal Service

Allow me to explain once again the soul wisdom on universal service and our virtue.

Virtue is a spiritual currency, just as money is on a physical plane.

Unlike money, the virtue stays with the soul eternally.
In other words, virtue expands and grows our soul power.

There is nothing more potent than the power of the soul for our collective or individual existence.
When we offer good service, genuinely without expecting anything in return, we receive a wealth of virtue for our journey.

When we do something for recognition or fame, we are less blessed. Our ego and attachment to that cause are stopping the flow and virtue to come our way.

Also, for money, we cannot by virtue.
The reason that many wealthy and some people do not experience true happiness and abundance is they lack virtue.

Spiritual wisdom is, we earn virtue for our journey specifically by creating a good cause through service.

Therefore, the law of universal service is:

- Serve a little; receive a little virtue from the Universe, the Divine, and the Source.
- When we serve more, we receive more virtue.
- Unconditional service, when we do not expect rewards, creates unlimited virtue for our journey.

Thus, the unconditional silent service is the gold for our evolution. It is when we benefit the lives of others and our own the most.

We can join as one in this practice by inviting others to our practice. When we invite others, their soul will gladly join us, thus we benefit them on the soul level. We are all connected in the quantum field of creation and the Ascension high-frequency light field.
Our higher self presence is in action through the breath, love, and light, we are transmitting to the grid. Activated, the Ascension field is blessing all in return.
Let us join hearts and souls to assist humanity, Mother Earth, and our lives to evolve further!

Working With The Ascension Grid And The Activation Meditation Practice

In essence, we will connect our body through energy centers with the Ascension grid to receive upgrades to our current state and frequency.

Stand up straight. You can also sit in a chair or on the floor. Make sure your spine is straight and away from any surface, allowing light to flow.

Relax. Take a few deep breaths to your lower abdomen and slowly exhale.

On the exhale, imagine all you do not need is leaving you and relaxing you even more.

Begin by inviting all light workers of the world and humanity to join the practice and accelerate with you. **Visualize everyone as a myriad of light bulbs around the globe in meditation together.**

Send the grounding cord of light to the core of the Earth.

The crystal core of the earth is responding by giving love and light to your Earth Star chakra.

At the same time, visualize the light force of the universe through your cosmic portal is coming down.

Shiva/Shakti, creation and manifestation energy and light are running through your central channel in a column of crystalline white light.

Visualize your Earth Star chakra and all seven chakras lighting up one-by-one.

Take another deep breath to the Earth Star chakra, seeing it light up. Intentionally on an exhale, stream the light and love up to the Ascension grid.

Visualize the ascension grid lights up while releasing the I AM crystalline frequency and light to you and

many people on earth.
Feel and see the masses awakening to their I AM presence.
Stay with this visualization for a minute.

Connecting Our Energy Centers With The Light-Ascension Field

Continue now to focus on the First Chakra. Visualize the ruby-red vortex of light rotating counter-clockwise and expanding. The crystalline frequency of your foundational energy is strengthening your being.
Take a deep breath, while exhale send the light up to the Ascension grid.

Ask for assistance and what you need help with at the moment.
See the ascension-field lighting up like a wildfire streaming down light-frequency and codes to you and those you invited on earth.
Stay for a minute in the feeling nature of this experience.

When ready, visualize the bright orange light in your Second Chakra. See the light, through its center expanding throughout the body in a counter-clockwise motion. The body is turning into a bright-orange force of your creative powers in purpose.

Send the rays of light and love in action to the Ascension grid. **When activated, the grid is streaming down the light, awakening and igniting the creative powers for all.**
Repeat the process for all chakras and receive benefits by spending a few minutes on each.

Visualize the golden wheel in the solar plexus, rotating and connecting you with the power of your soul. Imagine your sun here, expending its golden rays of light up to the

Ascension grid. The grid is activating. See the ascension light coming down and increasing the soul power for everyone we previously invited.

Visualize all people empowered by this network of light, shining like the million suns around the **globe.**

Stay with this visualization for a moment.

Ask For A Transformation You Desire And See It Coming To You And Others

Continue up and focus on the middle of your chest in the heart center. Send love and light from your heart chakra up to the Ascension grid. Initiated by love from your heart, the grid rains down the higher frequency of love and light to you and more people on earth.

The ascension light is bringing love, balance, and harmony to the hearts of many, awakening to their gifts and talents.

Visualize Mother Earth and humanity awakened and bathed in love and light from the Ascension grid.

Through breath, wake opens your Higher-Self heart and stream up your unconditional love for all to the grid.

Feel the power of this higher-self love activating the Ascension grid. The grid responds by streaming down Christ's unity consciousness to you and all. See more people are awakening to unity consciousness.

See people elated and free through the power of this ascension love and light.

In your throat, visualize the vortex of sky-blue light, now spinning and emitting its crystalline light to the Ascension grid. The ascension frequency light is coming down and initiating many to their truth. **Receive the codes on how best to shine your light and speak your truth.**

Imagine many people awakening through their purpose. Stay with this visualization for a moment.

Now, in the center of your brain, visualize indigo blue flame streaming its high-frequency waves up to the Ascension grid.
The ascension light field is responding and bringing a high-frequency intuitive knowledge and awareness to you and many.

Take a breath through this visualization of more people awakening and advancing through their spiritual channels.

Embodying The Higher Realms Of Consciousness & Awareness

When you are ready, see your Crown Chakra opening in crystalline translucent violet light, emitting light to the Ascension grid.
The grid is lighting up while pouring down the higher frequency light to all present.
The light is opening the crown chakras to more people and connecting them to the higher realms of consciousness and awareness and their multidimensional being. .

Ask for assistance for your journey and receive the messages.

In the end, thank the Ascension grid and all souls who came to practice, and send them back to their abroad by saying:
For all those who came please, return, get well, get perfect.
Thank you, thank you, thank you. Love you, love you, love you.
The first thank you is for the Divine, the Source, countless planets, stars, galaxies, and universes. The second thank

you is for the Ascension grid, and the third thank you is to your soul.

May we all benefit from working with the Ascension grid and accelerate further collectively and individually.

27

A Vision Of The New Earth

We have come to an end of this manual, yet it is only the beginning of our journeys of expansion and exploration in polishing the light within us and of the outer world.

By now, we all know, as the sun shines today, we will all have the opportunity to live and experience our higher selves potential, and purpose in this New Earth and the New Era we are co-creating together with all humanity, Mother Earth, and countless planets, stars, galaxies, and universes.

Keep your vision of the New Earth shine bright at all costs. Never underestimate and doubt your capability to contribute to making this world a better place.

Let us begin!

About The Author

Awaken The Light Within

My name is Tat Jane Bego Vic; I am a Certified Soul Teacher and Soul Song, Movement, and Dance Practitioner.

Since 2017, I am the founder of the wellness and awakening company, Soul Light Universal, in NYC.
Currently, I am looking for the opportunity and like-hearted visionaries to join forces and expand the essential wisdom, knowledge, and teachings for our new model of reality, in the New Earth and our evolution to the higher states of consciousness and awareness to more people nationwide and worldwide.
Primarily, I am a humanitarian, the truth seeker with a deep desire, through my work, to bring light to the world.

My seeker spirit in pursuit to positively impact human evolution brought me to New York City, where I live for most of my life. New York City's energy, passion, and multi-cultural environment opened my heart to its fullest and inspired me in every way.

In the journey of discovery and my pursuit to make difference by bringing more light to the world, I started as a singer/songwriter and co-founder of Bego Energizing Art in the mid-nineties in the city that never sleeps.
The concept of Bego Art was the creation of art that would not only be decorative and beautiful but would also help people focus and realize their higher self-potential and purpose. Some of the paintings can be viewed and purchased in a digital format in our Etsy store today.
My late sister Marijana's paintings and my music and songs, written at the time, were to energize and uplift the hearts and minds of people and bring them to their higher state and potential.

Over the years of being an artist, I realized that my music and pursuing the art world are not going to fulfill the intent of my life. Consequently, I turned my focus to the world within and studies, discovering my higher-self calling and potential to ignite the light within others now, through the awakening of the powers from within.
After a decade of personal studies and five years of studying the Power of Soul with the Institute of Soul Healing and Enlightenment, I founded the Soul Light Universal healing, transformation, and awakening company in 2017.
The Soul Light Universal holds groundbreaking knowledge and methods to empower and liberate people from the limitations to what is possible on our healing, transformation, and expansion journeys today.

Brings joy to my heart to acknowledge that current higher frequencies of light have lifted off much darkness from the Earth. The old world is dissolving in turbulence, and the New Earth is rising globally.

Most people are ready to evolve and relearn how to grow the light within and bring their higher-self potential and powers back.

So am I, to assist as many people in recognizing and overcoming the limitations of their current state and lead them to the awakening in purpose. When after to the higher states of consciousness and awareness, already present on Earth for our integration.

The Manual For Humanity Thriving In The New Earth, my first book, is here to assure that no one is left behind on the path of awakening and realization within.

Ultimately, to gather as many people to join forces in co-creating the new life and world on Earth, based on excellence, love, care, and cooperation.

In Love and Light,
Tat Jane Bego Vic
05.24.2021
New York, NY

To learn about our extraordinary: and unique teachings and services visit our website at:
https://soulightuniversal.com
email: t.j.bego@gmail.com
or write to:
Soul Light Universal
44 E 92nd Street
New York, NY 100128

.

Made in the USA
Middletown, DE
30 January 2022

60035607R00130